SOLUTION-ORIENTED THERAPY FOR CHRONIC AND SEVERE MENTAL ILLNESS

Bill O'Hanlon

AND

Tim Rowan

W. W. Norton
New York London

W. W. Norton & Company has been independent since its founding in 1923, when William Warder Norton and Mary D. Herter Norton first published lectures delivered at the People's Institute, the adult education division of New York City's Cooper Union. The Nortons soon expanded their program beyond the Institute, publishing books by celebrated academics from America and abroad. By mid-century, the two major pillars of Norton's publishing program—trade books and college texts—were firmly established. In the 1950s, the Norton family transferred control of the company to its employees, and today—with a staff of four hundred and a comparable number of trade, college, and professional titles published each year—W. W. Norton & Company stands as the largest and oldest publishing house owned wholly by its employees.

For information about permission to reproduce selections from this book, write to Permissions, W. W. Norton & Company, Inc., 500 Fifth Avenue, New York, NY 10110

Production Manager: Benjamin Reynolds
Manufacturing by Courier

Library of Congress Cataloging-in-Publication Data

O'Hanlon, William Hudson.
Solution-oriented therapy for chronic and severe mental illness / Bill O'Hanlon and Time Rowan.—[Rev. ed.]
    p. cm.
    Previously published: Solution-oriented therapy for chronic and severe mental illness / Tim Rowan and Bill O'Hanlon. New York: Wiley, 1999.
Includes bibliographical references and index.
ISBN 0-393-70423-8 (pbk.)
1. Mentally ill—Rehabilitation. 2. Solution-focused therapy. I. Rowan, Tim, 1952-. II. Rowan, Tim, 1952-. Solution-oriented therapy for chronic and severe mental illness. III. Title.

RC480.53.R69 2003
616.89'1—dc21   2003042068

W. W. Norton & Company, Inc.
500 Fifth Avenue, New York, N.Y. 10110
www.wwnorton.com

W. W. Norton & Company Ltd.
Castle House, 75/76 Wells St., London W1T 3QT

1 2 3 4 5 6 7 8 9 0

WITHDRAWN

SOLUTION-ORIENTED
THERAPY FOR
CHRONIC AND SEVERE
MENTAL ILLNESS

Books by Bill O'Hanlon
With Norton Professional Books

A Brief Guide to Brief Therapy
(with Brian Cade)

A Guide to Inclusive Therapy

A Guide to Possibility-Land
(with Sandy Beadle)

An Uncommon Casebook
(with Angela Hexum; currently out of print)

Even From a Broken Web
(with Bob Bertolino)

In Search of Solutions
(with Michele Weiner-Davis)

Love is a Verb (with Pat Hudson);
paperback version: *Stop Blaming, Start Loving*

Rewriting Love Stories
(with Pat Hudson)

Solution-Oriented Hypnosis
(with Michael Martin)

Taproots

A NORTON PROFESSIONAL BOOK

For Steffanie, who knows about patient persistence; for my Irish ancestors, who gave me faith, a love of words, and persistence in the face of hopelessness; for Patrice, who knows that there is a jewel in the garbage.

B. O'H.

Dedicated with love and gratitude to the memory of my mother, Colleen Rowan (1931–1994), and to the spirited nature and affection of my dad, Joseph Albert Rowan, Jr.

T. R.

ACKNOWLEDGEMENTS

I WANT TO THANK my clients for the honor and privilege of learning from them and for being so patient with me. Together we did our best and persevered to make their lives better.

I would like to thank the following persons for their helpful comments on the various drafts of this book as well as for their encouragement and support: Jay Haley, Bob Grooms, Linda Sowers, Amy Shuman, Delores Gengerich, and Dan Merlis.

Special thanks and appreciation to Carla Rowan, Cherie Snyder, and Ken Stewart for their tireless dedication to this book and the people it serves and to Charlene Ruffo who typed the original manuscript.

T.R.

PREFACE

*I*N THE MID-1970s, *as beginning clinicians, we were surprised and disillusioned with the pervasive pessimism of traditional thought when it came to helping those with "tough" problems—people with a history of psychiatric problems and inpatient treatment. Perhaps our relative lack of psychiatric training protected us from the implicit discouraging ("Don't expect any change; the best we can do is manage the illness") messages contained within traditional treatment theories and institutions. Like many new clinicians, we were naive and optimistic. For many reasons, however, we have never gotten over our optimism when faced with these tough problems (although we have become less naive as the years have passed). When we work with people, we don't see them through the lens of traditional theories, diagnoses, and prognoses; we only see people desperately in need of hope and change.*

This book, therefore, is about an *optimistic* set of methods and ideas that took shape over the years to successfully meet the needs of those people. We entered the field with a belief that even people with long-standing problems (so-called chronic, severe, and persistent mental illnesses) could change. Our experience over the intervening years has only confirmed this belief, as reflected in the concepts and cases presented in this book.

Over the years, we have learned much in collaboration with the people this book is about. In general, success demanded the ability to foster competence, empower individuals and families, instill a sense of control, communicate acceptance, create a context of cooperation, and transform problems into opportunities. In a climate of respect, trust, and hope, we *can* engender a healing, therapeutic atmosphere. Such an orientation is important in work with every client, but it is imperative for success with long-term, difficult cases. With this view of human nature—and a patient and relentless pursuit of change—many "impossible" cases can move from "maladjustment" toward psychological health and well-being.

The implications of this hopeful approach are profound. We use the designation of "tough" problems in recognition of the challenge that these cases present to both clients and clinicians. They are tough, but not impossible or intractable. They represent a serious challenge to those who adhere to traditional perspectives. At the same time, they sow seeds of hope for others who are searching for a more health-oriented approach.

THE POWER AND IMPACT OF BELIEF SYSTEMS: IATROGENIC DISCOURAGEMENT AND IATROGENIC HOPEFULNESS

Therapists' and clients' beliefs about treatment methods—and the expected results—have a direct and powerful impact on the outcome of therapeutic transactions (Fish, 1974; O'Hanlon & Weiner-Davis, 1989; O'Hanlon & Wilk, 1987). Whether or not they are helpful, belief systems have the power to inhibit alternate views. Once beliefs are taught and learned as though they are reality, people often rigidly adhere to them, as if other possibilities do not exist.

For people with tough problems and a lifetime of unfortunate learning and discouraging messages and labels, there is little hope within the constraint of traditional psychiatric belief systems. But when theory does not support the goal of therapeutic change, it should be challenged and then abandoned or extended in favor of more productive theoretical assumptions and working methods.

Over time, we have become increasingly convinced that traditional pathological language, labels, belief systems, and treatment methods can inhibit positive change. In fact, a hopeless situation can be engendered with unintentional and unfortunate cues from treatment milieus, therapists, family members, and oneself. *Iatrogenic discouragement—* that which is inadvertently induced by treatment—is often the result of such an unfortunate view of human perception and behavior. The impact of inpatient psychiatric treatment and a pathological view increases the probability of iatrogenic illness and discouragement through stigmatization, self-deprecation, and chronicity. Our approach seeks to avoid iatrogenic harm and, instead, to create iatrogenic health and healing.

THERAPY AS PARTNERSHIP: SHARING GROUND WITH THE HOPELESS

The most unusual—yet most powerful—aspect of our journey to forge hopeful solutions to tough problems was that the core concepts of the approach detailed here evolved primarily in collaboration with our clients. Indeed, we found this collaboration essential. Many of our colleagues were not receptive to our "irreverent" concepts, so we turned to clients for their input and perspective on how to work with them and how to identify what had not been helpful in past treatments. They responded very favorably to such respectful treatment. Once, when Bill was frustrated while treating a family with many problems, he asked them why they continued coming to see him, when he was not really helping them that much. They replied, "You're the first person who hasn't treated us badly and been angry at us. You seem to like us." Generally, we like our clients and, without exception, we treat them as people, not as diagnoses or biochemical constellations.

We have found that when we let a client in on what we are thinking and doing—a "no-no" in many of the theories we were taught—a healthy reciprocity is created. Feedback is welcomed and incorporated. Such a context of cooperation empowers clients to discover and use more of their existing potential and abilities, as they strive to regain power and control over their lives. This type of partnership is at the core of the successful treatment of tough clients that this book demonstrates.

Within the idea of therapy as collaboration lies a hopeful orientation in which both parties contribute areas of expertise. The therapist simply functions in the role of a facilitator (or possibly an initiator) who meets people where they are and then introduces options for changes in thinking, perception, or action. Clients' responses indicate acceptance or rejection of the changes that have been introduced. This leads to a dialectical process: the therapist in turn responds to the client's responses.

Tough clients—persons with serious psychiatric problems—do not change easily. When they do achieve positive changes, maintaining those changes requires continuing attention to circumstances that threaten to initiate old emotional reactions and unworkable patterns. Peeling away the barriers to change and unraveling the effects of past conditioning are tasks that demand extreme patience.

Our work is characterized by a relentless effort to discover and implement needed changes, even in the face of repeated "failures." We have also learned that varying time commitments are necessary to help initiate and maintain therapeutic change. Some of the cases in this book illustrate brief therapy, others are long-term, and a few are examples of serial brief therapy (a few initial sessions are followed by a break of several months or years, or irregular contact over the course of many years).

We are not attached to any specific length of therapy for these clients; rather, we let the needs of the specific case dictate the length of treatment. In other words, we put results and respect first, and we let these principles naturally guide what is effective and what promotes positive outcomes.

SEEDS OF HOPE/SEEDS OF CHANGE

This book offers a new and hopeful way to think about and intervene with those who have tough psychiatric problems or long histories of treatment. We offer an approach to therapy that emphasizes health, competence, and possibilities, instead of the traditional emphasis on pathology, deficits, and limitations (O'Hanlon & Weiner-Davis, 1989). Our approach also highlights methods by which therapists can help clients mobilize and develop their own resources to solve their own problems. At the same time, what you will read here is not a Pollyanna approach; we are dealing with difficult, life-threatening, and debilitating issues and struggles.

Some years ago, Dick Gregory, the comedian turned social activist, was asked whether he thought his hopes for eliminating hunger and starvation in the world could be achieved by the end of the twentieth century. He replied that he had once chanced on the scene of a building on fire. Firefighters were struggling to control the flames. Gregory asked the fire chief whether he thought he and his firefighters could save the building. The chief replied, "If there's a shift in the wind, we will. If not, we won't." Likewise, solution-oriented therapists who accept the challenge of working with tough clients must recognize the possibility that things won't change (the building might burn down). However, their work may prove to be the needed shift in the wind in a client's life.

TIM ROWAN
BILL O'HANLON

Cumberland, MD
Santa Fe, NM
August 1998

Preface to the Paperback Edition

*T*HIS BOOK'S DEVELOPMENT and publication in many ways parallels its subject matter.

Tim Rowan began working on what came to be titled *Solution-Oriented Therapy for Chronic and Severe Mental Illness* many years before I became involved with the book. Tim had worked with people who were struggling with severe behavioral and emotional problems, and he had become convinced that there were grounds for hope in therapeutic interventions. Although many clinicians despaired of making progress in these difficult cases, Tim discovered that there were possibilities for creative therapy and that very few of these possibilities had been detailed in books or the professional literature.

I initially became involved with this book in the capacity as a reviewer of an early draft of the manuscript. The publisher considering the manuscript had sent Tim's work to myself and another reviewer, and I proposed that the work be published while making some recommendations for revision. Later I met Tim at a symposium organized by *The Family Therapy Networker*. I introduced myself as one of the anonymous reviewers of his manuscript and asked him how the work was going. Tim told me that, on the basis of my strong recommendation, the publisher had been ready to give him a contract. At that point, however, the editor who had championed Tim's manuscript left the publishing house and the project was set aside. Upon hearing this news, I encouraged Tim to persist with the project. I believed that this was an important book, and I gave him a few leads with other publishers. If he still had trouble finding a place for the book, I then told Tim to contact me and that I would write him a letter of recommendation that might help get the manuscript published.

After our meeting at the *Family Therapy Networker* symposium, I forgot all about Tim's manuscript. Tim, however, went to work. A few years later, after he had taken the manuscript through many revisions and, again, at the point where he was very close to getting a contract, Tim contacted me. Unfortunately, for one reason or another, the early agreements with this second publisher also came apart. These disappointments led me to make the momentous (if slightly foolhardy) decision to offer to help rewrite the manuscript. With a little polishing, oriented toward highlighting Tim's inspiring and moving case examples, I was sure that the work would appear in print.

Much to my chagrin, Tim took me up on my offer. (He is, as you will discover in reading this book, a gently persistent and persuasive character). And so, with my collaboration, the book was further revised and, finally, published.

Now we are pleased to release *Solution-Oriented Therapy for Chronic and Severe Mental Illness* in paperback. We hope the book will have a new life in this form—that it will reach an even wider audience of readers and that the benefits of our therapeutic work will be shared by a greater number of therapists and clinicians.

How does this story of the writing, rewriting, and publication of this book parallel the spirit of and methods presented in these pages? With the population of people with chronic and severe mental illnesses, therapy does not always go smoothly or well. But these difficulties offer therapists no reason to give up and retreat to the reassuring (but false) idea that therapy will not work with this group. Persistence, creativity, and hope go a long way to achieving success. Even in the face of the most discouraging of moments, taking the long view helps both therapist and clients.

Tim and I are both persistent, incorrigible optimists. We hope you are too. Or that you become one by the time you finish this book.

Bill O'Hanlon
Santa Fe, NM
December 2002

CONTENTS

CONTENTS

SOLUTION-ORIENTED THERAPY FOR CHRONIC AND SEVERE MENTAL ILLNESS

CHAPTER ONE

A Hopeful Approach to Chronic and Severe Mental Illness

*T*WO DECADES AGO, TIM *began work at a state inpatient psychiatric facility. Fresh out of social work training, he
had limited field experience. Tim learned (from senior and
more experienced staff members) that schizophrenia was in-
curable and that persons with the disorder were in and out of
touch with reality. Furthermore, such patients would have
psychotic episodes periodically for the rest of their lives. On
one unit of the state hospital was a self-absorbed, "schizophrenic" man who, occasionally, would act as if he were a
rooster. When this happened, he was considered to be "psychotic" and out of touch with reality. One day, he requested
Tim's assistance in making formal arrangements for the bur-
ial of a loved one. For several days, he worked closely with
Tim, at no time behaving unusually. He provided relevant
phone numbers, names, and places, and actively participated
in every negotiation, even those involving complex monetary
transactions. Afterward, he returned to his self-absorbed state
and his rooster impressions. At that time, his ability to make
such rapid shifts from one state to another perplexed Tim.*

Several years later, on a different ward within the same
hospital, Tim's experience with another patient showed
him that change was possible for this population. Around
this time, Tim was reading *Uncommon Therapy: The Psychiatric Techniques of Milton H. Erickson* (Haley, 1973),
which narrated how Erickson creatively intervened with a
young woman who thought her feet were too big and was
too ashamed of them to be around others. Milton Erickson
worked in state psychiatric facilities before the advent of
today's "miracle" medications, so he approached patients

as a *therapist*. Because he was such a pragmatic, goal-oriented therapist, he developed hopeful and creative approaches that were quite successful with challenging and chronic clients. Tim took inspiration from Erickson in his work with "Big Ears."

Big Ears

James, a young man classified as paranoid schizophrenic, was admitted involuntarily to an inpatient admission ward of a state psychiatric hospital. He was very angry and not cooperative in giving information to staff. His mother indicated that he was very idealistic and unwilling to work for others who told him what to do. He lived with her and spent the day wandering around, doing as he pleased. James had a quick temper and did not get along with his father, who had remarried after the parents' divorce. In addition, James obsessively dwelt on the idea that his ears and nose were too big.

One day, while I was seeing James individually, he was preoccupied. I had to repeat my point several times before he responded. Taking a cue from Erickson, I said in a loud and harsh tone of voice, "If you had bigger receptors, I would not have to repeat myself so frequently." James's head jerked back, and he looked at me as if he were stunned. After a minute, during which he stared ahead and seemed even more self-absorbed, I changed the topic and quickly ended the session.

Two weeks later, I was surprised and pleased when his mother told me that her son was no longer concerned about his ears.

Although James still had many other problems—including a fixation on his nose—the brief therapeutic encounter with him showed Tim that change was possible, if only the therapist pulled the correct lever. Erickson's work offered the promise of just such a lever.

While Tim was experimenting with Ericksonian approaches with patients in the state hospital, Bill was using Ericksonian methods and ideas in drug and alcohol treatment settings, as well as outpatient mental health. He occasionally had the opportunity to treat psychosis and challenging psychiatric problems. As demonstrated by Mary's story below, Bill also found that "tough" clients responded well to these creative interventions.

"Mary, Mary!" "What?"

I once saw a 38-year-old woman who reported that her father had sexually abused her when she was very young. When she confronted him, he denied the abuse. She began hearing voices and was hospitalized for seven years. After her release from the hospital (her insurance carrier had finally refused to pay for any more treatment), she went to live with her parents, since she could not afford to live elsewhere. Her father agreed to pay for her outpatient treatment and medications. When we discussed the possibility of her moving into her own place, her main concern was that she would not be able to afford the medications (I was willing to forgo my fee until she got on her feet financially). I asked her why she was on medications and she answered that she was psychotic and needed to be on them. I asked what the medications were supposed to be taking care of specifically and she said they were to eliminate her hallucinations. I asked her to tell me about the hallucinations and she said that she had in the past seen people in her family walk by her when she knew that in reality they were in a different city. She had not had any visual hallucinations for some years, however, and now only heard voices. When asked what the voices said, she replied, "They only say my name, 'Mary.'" When I asked her whether the medications had eliminated the voices or had helped her cope with them, she said they hadn't. I had an idea, I said, that might help with the voices and might help her get off medications, so she would be more able to live on her own.

When I was in high school, I lived in the attic of my family's house. We had lots of kids, and the oldest one got to live in his or her own room, far away from the rest of the family. I loved this room for its privacy. But my mother hated it because I wasn't very good at getting up in the morning. She would come to the bottom of the steps to the attic and call up for me to get out of bed, as I was running late. "Bill!" she would call. "I'm up," I would reply, and just lie there and go back to sleep almost instantly. Ten minutes later, she would notice I was not downstairs and again would call, only this time a bit louder. "Bill!!!" "Yeah, sorry; I fell back to sleep. I'm up now." But again I would lie there and fall asleep. The third time was the charm, in part because my mother's voice tone and volume would rise to a level that, I knew, meant business. "BILL!!!!!!" Finally, I would get up.

After I told Mary this story, I suggested that maybe the voices were trying to get a response from her or trying to communicate something to her. I asked her whether she had ever replied when the voices cried, "Mary." She smiled slightly at the suggestion and answered that she had never thought of that, but she agreed to try it between sessions.

When she returned for the next session, I asked her whether she had asked the voices what they wanted. She said that when they had called her name, she had (in silence) replied, "What?" They had merely repeated her name, louder, "Mary!!!" "What?!" she had replied. "MARY!!!!!!" "WHAT?!!!" "Stay," the voices had said. I was crestfallen. The voices seemed to be telling her to stay in her parents' home. But before I leaped to any hasty conclusions, I decided to ask her, "What do you think that meant?" She replied, "They were telling me to stay in therapy. My father is pressuring me to leave therapy because he knows we are talking about sexual abuse in here." "So, do you think the voices can be helpful at times?" I asked. "Yes," she replied. There was more work to do, but that was a turning point in the work we did together.

These and other experiences showed us that there were therapeutic possibilities with difficult psychiatric cases. But prevailing theories offered little explanation or guidance in this area. The situation reminded us of the story of the skeptical Scottish engineer who, upon seeing the first steam engine, said, "OK, it works in practice, but does it work in theory?" We knew that what we were doing worked in practice, but did it work in theory?

Tim and Bill began corresponding and talking, after meeting in the early 1980s. We discovered a mutual interest in Milton Erickson's work. When we discovered our mutual belief that challenging and difficult psychiatric cases could be approached in a more hopeful way, we decided to collaborate in articulating the theory behind our approach and writing about it in a way that would make it available to others. Tim, who has specialized in working with this population, supplied much of the case material, and Bill supplied additional case illustrations and help with the writing. We are passionate about working in respectful and effective ways with these "tough" clients and are on a mission to share these ideas with others.

First, even though we don't favor initials or jargon, let's agree to use the shorthand CSMI for a person who is chronically or severely mentally ill. It's easier than spelling the words out each time. If you are put off by labels, think of these initials (as did one of our readers) as standing for clearly and substantially making improvements.

CSMI clients *can* improve. In fact, one of the first components of our work with CSMI clients involves challenging the ideas that mental health professionals, clients, and families have about the problem.

CHALLENGING THE BELIEF IN THE
IMPOSSIBILITY OF CHANGE

The first idea that we challenge is that of the impossibility of change. Common mental health folklore holds that schizophrenia and other chronic and severe mental problems are lifelong with no possibility of remission. We are convinced that the CSMI *can* change. There is much research that shows hope and possibility. Harding and Brooks (1984) reported that, in a 32-year longitudinal study, one half to two thirds of "chronic" patients who had been hospitalized in a state psychiatric hospital in Vermont had achieved significant improvement or recovery. Of those patients diagnosed as schizophrenic, 34 percent achieved full recovery in both psychiatric status and social functioning, and another 34 percent showed significant improvement in both psychiatric and social areas.

As solution-oriented therapists, we start with an assumption that the person may recover from the problem or that change in some areas can be affected by psychotherapy. Sometimes, our assumptions are proved wrong, but not before we make a persistent effort to help the person change. More often, our assumptions are warranted.

At this point, you may be thinking, "Boy, are these guys naive! They believe schizophrenia can be cured with psychotherapy." Stick with us. We operate from a rational but committedly optimistic model. We believe in the possibility of change, and we look for the place where change is *possible,* rather than where it is impossible. We want to help our clients focus on the areas in which the glass is half full. In different cases of CSMI, different possibilities for change are going to be available—even if the possibility is a matter of degree. If hallucinations are going to be regular recurrences throughout a person's life, we look for change in the frequency, severity, and interpretation of the hallucinations, and the relationship the person, the family, and the mental health professionals have to them.

CHALLENGING IDEAS THAT BLAME CLIENTS OR FAMILIES

Some years ago, the National Alliance for the Mentally Ill (NAMI), a consumer group comprised mostly of families of people with diagnoses of serious mental illness such as schizophrenia and manic depression, started objecting to family therapy as a treatment modality for severe mental illness. Their main concern was that families who entered such treatment often got the message that something about their family interactions or parenting had caused the relative's mental disorder. Families did not want to be blamed, however subtly, for something they believed they had not done. To be blamed is especially galling to families who have had their lives shattered and their finances compromised in attempting to care for and cope with their disturbed relative. Blaming can disconnect people with psychiatric disabilities from their families, when being connected is what they may need most. In response to their concerns, NAMI took the position that mental illness is an exclusively biological/neurological illness. This position, although understandable because it removes the blame from the family, is not the only way to avoid the unproductive blame game. Going to the biochemical extreme unnecessarily oversimplifies the issue and leaves only one possible intervention—medication. As anyone who has worked with people with chronic and severe mental illness knows, medications are not a magic cure-all. Many people do not take their medications, or they take them irregularly. Even those who do take their "meds" regularly and properly are not necessarily cured. Medications may not work; or, the side effects or long-term neurological impact of the medications may be as bad as or worse than the disorder itself. Sometimes, a medicine works only partially. Because family finances have often been taxed by housing, feeding, or rescuing the ill person when he or she gets into trouble (airline tickets home, bail, covering bounced checks or unpaid debts, and so on), medications can further drain a family's resources, and the expense can become prohibitive.

Family therapy got a bad reputation with NAMI families, but families obviously have a great deal of interest in getting information and help in dealing with their troubled relatives. In the 1980s, a "psychoeducational" approach gained popularity. Families were invited to a seminar in which they learned "facts" about mental illness and strategies for coping with their relative's disturbed behavior. Although psychoeducation is a positive development, families are often told that their relative's condition is "chronic" and can be expected to last for the rest of the relative's life. Like a bad hypnotic suggestion, this verdict can create iatrogenic (treatment-caused) problems.

CHALLENGING IDEAS THAT SEE CLIENTS AS NONACCOUNTABLE

Just as diabetes does not cause a person to eat sugar, CSMI does not cause a person to behave in any particular way. We view people with CSMI as capable of making choices about what they do. They may not be able to choose in regard to having a hallucination, but they can choose what they do when they have hallucinations. Not everyone who experiences hallucinations acts on them. Why not? Individual choice.

While working at a community mental health center, Bill was called to the reception area because one of his former clients had appeared and was "acting strangely," according to the receptionist. Bill had seen Tom (a likable, shy 19-year-old) for a few sessions two years previously. The focus of the therapy had been to help Tom overcome his fear of asking women out on dates. Here is Bill's narrative of the new encounter.

When Tom arrived in my office, he said that he was there because he had heard some disturbing things on the radio and television in the past few days, and he was upset by them. He'd been wandering the streets obsessing about the things he'd heard and getting more and more upset. He remembered that I had helped him before and decided to come to see me. He told me that he'd been hearing all sorts of strange things on the television and radio, but the most disturbing thing was what he had heard just this morning: a report during the morning radio news that he had bitten his brother's penis in half. He was very upset by this, and outraged that someone would say something that wasn't true and broadcast it to thousands of listeners. At other moments, he wondered whether he had indeed bitten his brother's penis in half. I told him that I had missed the news that morning, but that I doubted whether what he had heard had been broadcast. I thought it was a hallucination, a projection from his own mind onto the radio and the television. He considered my opinion for a moment and then said, "Do you really think so?" I assured him that I did. He was silent, but eventually agreed that I was probably right. I asked him whether he had ever had any other problems with hallucinations. He told me that he had been hospitalized and put on medications the previous year, after hallucinating in a similar way. I asked whether the medications had helped, and if so, why he had stopped taking them. He told me that they had helped, but they took a while to work; it had been good that he was able to be in the structured environment of the hospital for a few days, so he could settle down until the medications took effect. He had visited the hospital clinic as an outpatient for about six months after his release. Because he was no longer having hallucinations and the trip to the hospital was long and bothersome, he had stopped going back for regular visits and stopped taking his medications when the prescription ran out. He told me that if these were hallucinations, maybe he'd better get back on medications. He was afraid of what he might do if he was this upset. I asked him whether he thought it would be better for him to be in the hospital while he got back on the medications, or whether he thought he could cope while he was out of the hospital. He told me that he would rather be in the hospital. Together, we called the hospital and found out that they would be able to admit him that day. No one was available to help him get to the hospital, and he faced a wait of several hours for one of his family members to take him. After some discussion, we jointly decided that he was in good enough shape to take a bus to the hospital and admit himself. He called me from the hospital to let me know he had arrived, and I talked to the admitting psychiatrist.

Not everyone in Tom's condition would be well enough to recognize that he or she was having hallucinations, or to get himself or herself to the hospital alone (and we wouldn't generally recommend such a course, due to liability and other concerns). The point of the story is that people are often more accountable, even in the midst of psychotic episodes, than we give them credit.

We have found that focusing on those aspects of their lives where clients have choices increases their sense of accountability and of what the philosophers call "personal agency." Personal agency means that the person feels himself or herself to be an active agent in life, rather than a passive victim of life. Social psychologists call this "efficacy."

CHALLENGING IDEAS THAT DISEMPOWER OR
INVALIDATE CLIENTS OR FAMILIES

Bill had a client with severe obsessions (to the point of delusions and self-harm) who went into a general hospital's psychiatric ward when she was suicidal. While there, she developed a skin rash that started to grow worse day by day. Each day, she would complain about the rash to the psychiatrist, who would visit her during his daily rounds. She asked him to write an order for her to be able to see a dermatologist about the rash, since she wasn't allowed to leave the unit or request such a consultation directly while on the psychiatric unit. The psychiatrist told her that the rash was from her compulsive showering and that it would clear up on its own. She disagreed, telling him that she had compulsively showered for years, but had never had a rash like this. He still refused to write the order for a dermatological exam, even though the rash grew quite severe. When she finally got out of the hospital, she made an appointment with a dermatologist, who diagnosed eczema and gave her a prescription that promptly cleared up the rash and relieved her discomfort. The dermatologist told her that she should have gotten it treated long before it became so severe.

Although this is a dramatic example, it illustrates an all-too-common occurrence: invalidating CSMI clients' perceptions. We don't listen because we believe that their concerns are only another manifestation of the illness and have no basis in reality.

Mental health professionals do have some expertise in treating CSMI. And clients (and their families) are not experts on neurology, medication effects and dosage, change techniques, and so on. But clients, and families, do have their own areas of expertise, which therapists tend to ignore or stifle. They are experts on their experience with the problem. They are experts about what works and doesn't work in regard to the things that have been tried in the past. The expertise of clients and family members is a keystone of the solution-oriented approach to working with "tough" clients. The following case example illustrates tapping into a family's expertise to help a CSMI client.

Bill was consulted by a family whose 19-year-old daughter was approaching strange men on the street and offering to have sex with them. She was convinced that she was the Queen of the Moon and that she was to offer her sex to the mortals of Earth as a divine blessing. Unfortunately, even though she was clearly disturbed, some men took her up on the offer. Her family members would try to keep an eye on her so that she wouldn't wander away from home, but this became impossible when she was agitated. She would get very upset and run out of the house, biting and kicking family members who tried to restrain her. Medications had been tried, with little effect. Hospitalization was not helpful either, and the family was committed to caring for her at home. In talking to the family members, we focused on what helped to calm her down when she became agitated. During this discussion, it became clear that, often, one or more of the family members would try to physically restrain her, or would get upset and raise their voices with her when she became unruly. She would invariably get more agitated when this happened. When I asked what seemed to calm her down, we discovered that when one of the female family members took her into another room, away from the others, and spoke to her in soft, soothing tones, she would often, though not always, calm down. The family then made a crisis plan that involved having her mother and/or sisters (who lived nearby) being available for times when the woman became agitated.

Table 1.1 summarizes the commonly held ideas that the solution-oriented approach challenges.

TABLE 1.1
IDEAS TO CHALLENGE ABOUT CSMI

Impossibility Ideas

❖ Clients can never recover from CSMI.

❖ There is nothing to do but manage these clients. They won't be able to make meaningful changes in their problems or their lives.

❖ Clients will need to be on medication for the rest of their lives.

Blaming Ideas

❖ The person's family has caused the CSMI.

❖ The client or the family is resistant.

❖ The client is playing games and doesn't really want to change.

❖ The client acts out because he or she wants and likes attention.

Nonaccountability Ideas

❖ The client is ill, therefore he or she is unable to control or change his or her behavior.

❖ The client's behavior is determined by the CSMI.

Invalidating/Disempowering Ideas

❖ Clients and families don't know anything about CSMI. They need to be taught about it by mental health experts.

❖ CSMI is purely a neurological/brain disorder, and the only effective thing to do about it is to give medications.

❖ When clients or families have a complaint in connection with their situation (medications, side effects, upsetting contacts with treatment personnel, medical issues), it is a reflection of their illness and not a "real illness."

Summary Points
Chapter One

❖ Therapy is possible even with chronic, severe, and persistent "mental illness."

❖ Respect, creativity, collaboration, and effectiveness are keystones to this approach.

❖ Milton Erickson, working with psychiatric "patients" before the discovery of drug treatments, developed creative and effective approaches. The approaches detailed in this book are based in part on Erickson's methods and spirit.

❖ This chapter was meant to inspire the reader and to give a sense of what this approach is about. In later chapters, we'll get more specific about the how-tos and the theory behind our solution-oriented approach.

CHAPTER
TWO

Riding the Wave

*S*INCE THE LATE NINETEENTH *century, much has been made of the biological basis for severe and chronic mental illnesses such as schizophrenia, severe depression, and manic depression. When some medications were found to be helpful in managing the symptoms of such disorders, it was hailed as proof that the disorders had a biological basis. This is akin to arguing that if you take cocaine and it helps lift your depression, you have a biological disorder involving cocaine deficiency. Time may show that there is a clear biological basis for these severe mental disorders, but the scientific jury is still out on what the causes are.*

In the meantime, we propose a state-based biological model for understanding and treating severe and chronic mental illness. This "state-fluctuation" view holds that people have fluctuations in their biochemical and neurological states, and these fluctuations can influence the severity and course of their problems. Various external and internal elements can influence state changes. A surge of a hormone might trigger someone into a psychotic state. A stressful life event, or problems with intimates, might trigger depression. Poor nutrition might trigger manic activity.

Conversely, a client who has a hormonal surge might have learned some preventive measures to make sure that a full-blown psychotic state did not follow. Exercising every day during times of stress may have been identified as a way to reduce the symptoms of depression. A change of diet that eliminates sugar and adds more vegetables may help when the signs of an impending episode begin to appear.

The point is, severe psychiatric problems do not manifest to the same degree at all times. Symptoms fluctuate, and that fluctuation, although seen by many as indicative of problems, is what gives us hope. Our approach is to help the person (and his or her family) to notice and use the best of what works to lessen the symptoms or cope with them in the best way, thereby triggering better biochemical, psychological and emotional states. Jason's experience with a demon lover illustrates this technique of "riding the wave" of fluctuation.

The Devil's Penis

Bill consulted on a case in which a young man, married only a few years, had become convinced that the devil was visiting him every night and having anal sex with him. It had all started, Jason said, after their child was born and his wife started sleeping in the living room. She was a seamstress and would doze and work throughout the night, so she started to sleep in cat naps in the living room. All alone in their bedroom, Jason was visited one night by a spirit, he told me, that had begun to perform oral sex on him. Because he and his wife had not had sex for some time, he was happy for the visitation, even though he felt a little guilty about betraying his wife with the spirit. The spirit began to visit quite regularly, but gradually became more and more violent with him, sometimes hurting his penis by biting and sucking it so hard. He started to resist, but alas, it was too late. The spirit had developed some sort of power over him and could do things to him even without his consent. He became frightened and went to the library one day to look up some information about spirits. He found that the spirit who was visiting him was probably a succubus, and that it came from the devil. He was very frightened when

he learned this, and sought the advice and help of his minis-
ter. The minister, a very wise and gentle man, reassured him
that it was most probably a psychological and emotional issue
related to his marital problems. He urged Jason to talk to his
wife and sort out their difficulties. Jason did confess to his wife,
who was concerned but also understanding. For a time, the
nightly visits stopped and the couple began having sex on a
more regular basis. But one night, the wife was working on a
project, and the spirit visited again—more malevolent and in-
trusive than ever. It began to penetrate Jason's anus with what
felt like a burning hot penis. He resisted, but to no avail. Jason
was raped anally that night and regularly in the nights that
followed. The penis began to travel up his colon and wrapped
itself around his heart. He became terrified that he would have
a heart attack, and began having trouble breathing during the
attacks. He again sought out his minister and also talked to
his wife and his parents. The minister, at the urging of his par-
ents (who were convinced this was a spiritual problem), found
an exorcism prayer and said it for Jason. That relieved things
for a little while. But now the wife's parents, whom she had in-
formed, became involved. The in-laws were concerned for their
daughter's safety and were convinced that Jason had psycho-
logical problems that should be treated by a psychiatrist. A
struggle ensued between both sets of parents and the couple,
and soon the devil reappeared and the anal rapes began anew.
Jason was afraid to have sex with his wife now, because he
was afraid that the devil would enter his wife through him
while they were having sex. Finally, to appease his wife (and
her parents), he sought counseling.

He was fairly convinced that the devil was behind it all.
But he had considered that it might be a psychological prob-
lem. He just wanted help in having the attacks stop. He
claimed that he had once had his wife watch during an oral

sex episode with the spirit, and she confirmed that his penis had been moving as if he were having oral sex with someone who was not there.

I told him that I was not certain what the nature of the problem was. It might be of supernatural origins or it might be something else. My job was to find out what could help. Through some discussion, we found that four things seemed to diminish the likelihood of an attack:

1. *Having sex with his wife. The minister had assured him that since God had sealed the bonds of his marriage, the devil could not enter into them while they were having sex. The minister had therefore recommended that the couple have sex as often as possible to keep the devil at bay (see, he was very wise). They had recently been following his advice, and it had helped.*

2. *Saying the exorcism prayer had helped for a little while.*

3. *Talking to his wife and the minister about the visits helped. After he did so, the devil wouldn't visit that night. I asked whether telling me might have the same effect and he thought it might, since he felt less guilty and less frightened after he told me and I didn't criticize or coerce him. Talking with his parents or his in-laws was not helpful in the same way. In fact, when his parents and in-laws had become more involved, the visits were worse and more frequent.*

4. *One night, he got up out of bed as he was being raped and ran down the street (with his clothes on), and the devil hadn't seemed to be able to follow him and also didn't return that night.*

We made a plan to increase the four activities that helped. Soon after, the devil seemed to lose a grip on the young man. He also discussed the fact that his mother had had some sexual contact with him when he was a child and wondered whether this might have been a factor in bringing on the problem. The couple jointly decided to put some more distance between them and their parents.

Instead of focusing on Jason's "mental illness" or what caused it (was it biochemical, trauma-based, developmental, family-based, spiritual/religious?), we focused on:

1. What might help.

2. When the state fluctuates (in a positive and helpful direction).

PLACES AND WAYS TO SEARCH FOR
SOLUTIONS AND STATE FLUCTUATIONS

This section lists four methods you can use to help identify the times when the client's state fluctuates in the positive direction, and the actions or views that contribute to this positive swing. The idea here is not to convince clients that they have solutions and competence, but to ask questions and gather information in a way that convinces you and reminds them that they do experience better moments and have untapped strengths.

1. *Ask clients to detail times when they haven't experienced their problems when they expected they would.* Most clients and family members can recall times when the client

did better than usual in regard to the illness. Ask about the details of such occurrences. What are some possible reasons that things went better? How did others respond when the client was doing better? Was there ever a time when the usual problem started to occur but was interrupted, or didn't play itself out in the usual troublesome way?

Marcy, diagnosed as schizophrenic, was being cared for by her family. Hospitalization hadn't really helped her, and they were unwilling to institutionalize her. One particular problem was that her parents felt restricted from going out to eat, because of Marcy's disruptive behavior. They didn't like to cook at home all the time (they were both retired and enjoyed fine food), but hadn't been able to resolve this issue. When asked about a time when Marcy wasn't disruptive in a restaurant, they recounted a time when they went to a restaurant that let the patrons draw on the paper tablecloth. Marcy had been so absorbed in drawing all through dinner that she hadn't engaged in her usual behavior: yelling at the other patrons, laughing loudly at nothing at all, sliding under the table, and so on. It was decided that they would experiment with bringing a drawing pad, pencils, and crayons to their next outing. The dinner went smoothly, and future restaurant trips—in fact, any family outings—were always undertaken with art supplies at hand. The parents were able to do many more errands together, and they brought Marcy along. Previously, they had taken turns caring for her at home while the other parent did the errands alone.

2. *Find out what happens as the problem ends or starts to end.* Sometimes, aspects of what happens as the problem subsides can be used to decrease the frequency of the problem or to hasten its departure from the person's life. Usually, this involves discovering *actions* that are under the client's or

family's control and have spontaneously happened previously, and making those actions more deliberate during future occurrences of the problem.

Joe came in complaining about his hallucinations. He had been on medications, which at first had helped diminish the intrusiveness, although not the presence or frequency, of the hallucinations. He was having a tough time attending to his work and his studies (he was attending a community college). When Bill asked whether the hallucinations were always at the same level or were sometimes more intense, Joe said they came in waves. Sometimes they were so intrusive and vivid that he could barely attend to the outside world, and sometimes they were more in the background.

What did Joe do when he was coming out of a particularly intense bout of hallucinations and was beginning to be able to function more normally? Bill asked. Joe said that he would begin to listen to classical music on his stereo, and would go for a walk after he'd listened to music for a while and had calmed down. Bill suggested that Joe should listen to classical music during the most intense hallucinations and find out whether it helped him calm down. Joe found that the music calmed him enough that he could go for a walk. Joe was able to use this strategy to reduce the intrusiveness of the hallucinations by 50%.

3. *Investigate other contexts of competence.* You can often find out about moments of better functioning by asking about areas in the person's life that he or she feels good about—hobbies, areas of specialized knowledge, or well-developed skills. Other contexts of competence can be found if someone the client knows has faced a similar problem and has resolved it in a way that the client admires and wants to emulate.

Bill consulted with a colleague's client who was suffering from multiple personality disorder. She explained that various personalities would take over and wreak havoc in her life. She would sometimes "come to herself" miles away from her home and be late for an appointment, or for picking the children up from school, and so on. In the discussion, Bill asked about areas in which she felt competent. She told him that she made her living being a stage manager for the local theater company. Bill asked her to tell him what made her so good at it. She explained that actors are notoriously disorganized and temperamental, and she had a pleasant but firm way of keeping them organized and in sync with the entire production. Bill asked if she might be able to be an internal stage manager for all her personalities, ensuring coordination of necessary schedules and activities. She could arrange for whichever personality was needed to be "on stage" at the appropriate time. She found that this made a lot of sense and agreed to give it a try.

4. *Ask why the problem isn't worse.* This is a strange way of finding competence, but it often works. Compared to the worst possible state people could get into, how do they explain that their condition isn't that severe? This is like asking a 200-pound man why he doesn't weigh 300 pounds, when he claims his eating is out of control. You would find in his explanation the things he does to keep himself from weighing much more than 200 pounds. These things normalize the condition and restore perspective. But the important aspect of this inquiry is to track why or how the problem is contained, or what restraint keeps it from being worse than it is.

Marjorie, a client who had been sexually abused, was cutting herself on her thighs with a razor on a nightly basis. When,

during a session, she was asked how she had restrained her-
self from cutting on other areas of her body, she replied that
she did not want other people to see the cuts, so she kept the
cutting confined to her thighs, where no one would ever see it.
Persisting in the inquiry, the therapist told her he understood
her reason, but now wanted to know how she kept the cutting
confined. The ensuing discussion showed Marjorie that she
had some power and choices in relation to the cutting, and she
proceeded to challenge the cutting's demands that she hurt
herself every night.

CAPITALIZING ON CRISIS

Fluctuating emotional, biochemical, and psychological
states are akin to trances. Trance states are characterized by
some automatic behavior, thoughts, and feelings. Trances
can be creative and healing, or symptomatic, upsetting, and
unhelpful. Our work is designed to move people to more
helpful, functional trances. We do this by leveraging the
confusion and uncertainty that are present in the person
and the family during a crisis. Their confusion and uncertainty can be channeled in either direction. Instead of per-
ceiving crises as signs of impending decompensation, they
can be viewed as times to make a change from one state to
another. If the response to the crisis involves blame and
dire predictions of breakdown, the person, couple, or family may become more nonfunctional. These negative responses function as powerful posthypnotic suggestions
("You need to stay on your medications or you will never
get better!" "You are crazy!" and so on).

The following case, from Tim's practice, used this state
fluctuation concept. The client, who had experienced multiple hospitalizations, was able to stay out of the hospital.

Pierce had been hospitalized after he began telling his wife, and people he met on the street, that he had had a sexual encounter with a fictional woman he referred to as the "Queen of the South." Previously, he had only told his wife about this encounter while pacing back and forth in front of her, stating repetitively, "I'm damned."

Pierce was feeling as if his life was over. He had lost his job and was in danger of losing his marriage during the hospitalization. In the discussion Tim had with Pierce before he was discharged from the hospital, Pierce told Tim that part of the problem was that he did not control his drinking once he started, and he had become too involved with a cultish religious group, which led to his delusional thinking.

Before his hospitalization, Pierce had been working full-time as a stone mason. The analogy of a crumbling or crumbled wall came to mind. It was as if Pierce's dreams, and the life he had hoped for, organized, and built, had crumbled before his eyes because of the hospitalization and his wife's threats to leave him. Nevertheless, Tim pointed out that a man with expertise as a stone mason should know what action to take under such conditions (thus offering him a new, more helpful, view of his current situation). Pierce was then asked whether it was true that, when a wall made of stone crumbles or collapses, nothing is really lost. Was it not true that the essential elements or building components (rocks) maintain their natural integrity and structure, even if the binding material deteriorates. It was again implied that any stone mason would intuitively know what to do if a few rocks, or even a cornerstone (wife), were missing. He would simply chip off the old adhesive (cement), acquire additional building materials when necessary, design an updated structure, and then go about securing one stone at a time.

With Tim's help, Pierce began to make a list of the activities that would help him rebuild the wall and keep it from crumbling again. Here are some elements of the list:

1. *Stay away from alcohol. If you feel tempted, go to AA.*

2. *Find a different church to attend, one that isn't so intense and cultlike.*

3. *When you feel the urge to tell someone about one of your thoughts, which might be disturbing for that person, write it out first, and wait until you have a chance to discuss it with someone you trust (a counselor, or a close friend) before you tell anyone else.*

Pierce's mother called Tim one night some time later and said that Pierce was not talking; he was simply staring out into space. Tim agreed to meet the pair at the local ice cream stand. Pierce was led, unspeaking and staring blankly ahead, out of the car. Tim bought ice cream cones for them both and put one in Pierce's barely responsive hand. Tim reminded Pierce of their "stone wall" conversation and of the list of helpful actions they had come up with together. Would any of those things would be helpful now? Tim wondered. Pierce began to orient to the conversation and told Tim he was again having strange and disturbing thoughts that he felt compelled to tell others. It turned out that Pierce and his wife had just separated after a marital crisis, and his wife was talking seriously about divorce. Pierce had left their home and showed up in this disturbed state at his parents' home.

After telling Tim about the crisis, Pierce began to be more coherent and oriented. They went over the elements of the list, and Pierce agreed to stop drinking, to go to an AA meeting, and to write down his disturbing thoughts and bring them to an outpatient session that Tim scheduled for him. In this way, hospitalization was avoided.

Pierce and his wife did divorce, after several separations. At the time of this writing, Pierce has had twenty months of sobriety, attends AA regularly, and is working part-time once again.

WHAT DO YOU DO WHEN YOU DON'T LISTEN TO THE VOICES?

How does all this translate into clinical practice? Mostly, it involves (a) recognizing that clients fluctuate in and out of their problematic and resourceful states and (b) trying to decrease the things that trigger the problem states and increase the things that access or evoke the resourceful state. For example, if a client reports hearing voices that say hurtful or dangerous things, the therapist might ask what the client does when hearing voices but not attending to them or believing them. Most clients can identify what helps and what doesn't. We can help them and their family members use more of what helps and avoid the triggers that bring on the symptomatic states. Traditional approaches, which attend to the psychotic states more than the resourceful states, inadvertently reify and support psychotic states, which usually modulate from nonexistent to quite intrusive and severe.

SUMMARY POINTS
CHAPTER TWO

❖ People with chronic and severe mental illness (CSMI) fluctuate in the severity of their symptoms and impairment.

❖ This fluctuation is an alternative model for viewing the biochemical aspect of CSMI. It is seen as a constantly changing process, not as a fixed, set condition.

❖ The therapist can initiate and guide the search for moments or models of better functioning (state fluctuations), using the following four methods:

1. Ask clients to detail times when they haven't experienced their problems when they expected they would.

2. Find out what happens as the problem ends or starts to end.

3. Investigate other contexts of competence.

4. Ask why the problem isn't worse.

❖ Moments or times of crisis can be used productively to steer the person (and his or her intimates) in a more functional direction. Learn what helps evoke a different, more resourceful state, and mobilize the person and others to evoke that state deliberately.

CHAPTER THREE

*Rewriting Spoiled
Identity Stories*

*O*NE OF THE BIG *problems with CSMI is that people start to organize their view of themselves, and others' view of them, as their illness. Pathologized people behave pathologically. The job of the therapist is to help clients view themselves as capable and accountable members of society. Being treated with dignity can make all the difference, as it did for the client we call "Mrs. Terror."*

Mrs. Terror Becomes Queen Terror

The caseworker was at her wits' end. Two or three times a day, without an appointment, the woman would appear in the social services office, demanding to see her caseworker, Mrs. Johanssen. She would swear and bang things when told that she would have to wait, since Mrs. Johanssen was in a meeting, or with another client, or out to lunch, or absent that day. Other clients had learned to clear out of the waiting room. They had been hit, sworn at, or threatened by "Mrs. Terror," as this unkempt and wild woman had come to be known by all in the social services office.

When Mrs. Johanssen was finally available, Mrs. Terror would begin the meeting with a threat, yelling and banging around the office. Mrs. Johanssen had become a nervous wreak and was afraid of Mrs. Terror. Coming to work was getting harder and harder. In desperation, she brought the situation to Birgitta Hedstrom, the consultant for the social services, although she had little hope that Mrs. Hedstrom could offer any real help. Birgitta is a possibility thinker, but hearing about this situation was a challenge even to her optimism.

As she discussed the situation of Mrs. Terror with the entire staff, however, two intriguing features of the situation seemed to offer some possibilities. One was that even when she was swearing and threatening, Mrs. Terror always used the polite form of address: "Mrs. Johanssen," "Mrs. Ericsson," "Mrs. Andersson," and so on. (Most of the clients in social services called the staff by their first names.) The second interesting fact was that, although visits to Mrs. Terror's apartment revealed that it was generally a mess, with garbage, broken furniture, and clothing strewn about, she kept one beautiful Chinese vase intact and well cared for.

Birgitta became intrigued and asked more about Mrs. Terror. The staff said that she had come to Sweden from a place in another country that happened to also be the place of origin of the Queen of Sweden, who was much beloved by Swedes. Birgitta asked the staff to speculate about how they would treat the Queen if she happened to drop by unannounced one day. They laughed and quickly got into the fun of it. The receptionist, Mrs. Andersson, who had previously worked as a receptionist in a psychiatric hospital and could tolerate many unusual behaviors in a calm manner, was especially keen on this idea, so it was agreed that Mrs. Andersson would take on the task of making Queen Terror feel welcome the next time she appeared in the office. Mrs. Andersson prepared a special brew of nice coffee and kept it in a thermos next to her, along with two beautiful ceramic mugs she brought from home to substitute for the usual plastic foam cups used in the office.

When Queen Terror arrived, instead of the usual brusque manner she used with the woman, Mrs. Andersson quickly jumped up and greeted her like an old friend. "Hello," she said, "Welcome. I assume you've come to see Mrs. J. She's busy right now, but can I get you a cup of coffee while you are waiting?" Queen Terror appeared confused and uncertain in response to this atypical greeting. "Coffee would be nice, Mrs. Andersson," she said softly. When Mrs. Andersson appeared with the beautiful mugs of delicious coffee, she sat down and began to chat with the Queen about this and that. The Queen responded enthusiastically to this talk, and spoke quite normally. After her coffee was finished, she promptly announced that she did not need to see Mrs. Johanssen after all. "Are you sure?" asked Mrs. Andersson. "I'm sure she won't be long. Won't you please wait?" But the Queen waved her off. "No, it's OK."

On several succeeding days, this scene was repeated, with the same outcome. Soon, the Queen began to skip days and only show up on the day of her appointment. She was now behaving and speaking much more civilly.

During an appointment not long after, the Queen asked Mrs. Johanssen for her help in being able to keep her apartment. It seemed that she had previously terrorized many of the tenants with the same kind of behavior that she had showed at the social services office, and was being evicted. Mrs. Johanssen, impressed with the dramatic change in the Queen's behavior, agreed to be her advocate and intercede with the landlord. Mrs. Johanssen got the reluctant landlord to agree to a joint meeting at the social services office.

He arrived, belligerent, with a lawyer in tow, ready for the worst. But the Queen arrived and did not create the angry scene the landlord had expected. Instead, she softly told him that the eviction notice had caused her much pain. The landlord softened a bit and told her that he could understand that. She told him that it had also hurt her when he had gotten her committed twice to a psychiatric hospital. Tears ran down her face as she softly told him of the humiliation she had faced being taken away in front of the neighbors. He apologized for her pain, but said that he had felt it was the only option he had. She told him that she understood. She also said that she had visited every neighbor in the apartment building, asking them if they thought she deserved a second chance. They had

*unanimously agreed, and had also agreed to advocate for her
to the landlord if necessary. She also asked the landlord to
admit that many of the other tenants had behaved in a similar
manner, disrupting their neighbors' lives. He admitted that this
was true. Why was she being singled out then? she asked. The
landlord had no good answer for this. She asked him if he could
see his way to giving her a second chance. He agreed.*

*Mrs. Johanssen ended the meeting and called Birgitta Hed-
strom. "I now believe in miracles," she said. "I have seen one
today." Several years' follow-up has shown that, when treated
like a Queen, the former Mrs. Terror could behave with grace
and dignity. [This case example was from Birgitta Hedstrom,
Sundsvall, Sweden]*

One of the problems with earlier approaches to dealing
with CSMI was that people suffering from these problems
were sometimes put away from the mainstream of life and
became less able to function in the ordinary, everyday
world. They became stigmatized, shunned by "normal" people. Often, when they were put in psychopathic/psychiatric
hospitals, asylums, or rest homes, they developed institu-
tionalized mentalities. Erving Goffman, in his study of such
institutions and their inhabitants, called this stigmatizing
event the process of creating a "spoiled identity" for CSMI
people.

With deinstitutionalizing efforts, most of the chronic in-
stitutionalization has ceased, but people suffering with serious mental illness still become identified with their
diagnoses or the worst moments in their lives. They *become*
their problems. Instead of suffering from schizophrenia, they
become "a schizophrenic." Instead of suffering from manic
depressive disorder, they become "manic depressives." At
first, this may seem a trivial, semantic distinction, but living
a label can create a self-fulfilling prophecy.

In this chapter, we look at ways to destigmatize, de-pathologize, and separate people from their diagnoses. First, we will look at some general principles and methods for rewriting identity stories with CSMI people.

IDENTIFY A VALUING WITNESS

Search for people who do not view the client as disabled, incapable, or crazy. Discover—in the past or the present—people who can see beyond the problem to the person, or who can remember the person before the problem arrived in his or her life. We call this person, who can be an old friend or a family member, a "valuing witness." If the witness is available, we often invite him or her to a meeting, to get some evidence for a more hopeful and healthy view of the person. If the witness is not available in person, we hold "seances with the living"—we ask the client to stand in for the witness. For example, "If your best friend were here, what would he be able to tell me about the Jim who was here long before schizophrenia arrived in your life? What kind of person is *that* Jim?"

LOOK FOR HIDDEN STRENGTHS

Find out about hidden or nonobvious aspects of the person or the person's life that do not fit or are incompatible with his or her disempowered (hopeless, helpless, or stuck) views about self or the problem. As the person and/or his or her intimates how they explain the incompatibility.

When you listen with an attitude of hope and possibility, you'll often hear something during the course of an interview that contradicts the view that this person is out of control, can't change, isn't responsible, and so on. It's a bit like finding a picture of a polluted urban scene and noticing a pristine mountain lake in the middle of the photo. Train yourself to notice what is right with a picture (that is, what doesn't fit with the spoiled identity of the person with CSMI).

NORMALIZE AND DESTIGMATIZE

One of the insidious things about any chronic illness, especially mental illness, is that people begin to think of themselves as freaks who are different from others in a bad way. They begin to *feel* isolated and to actually *be* isolated. Connecting these folks with others who have experienced similar struggles, and have found alternative ways to think about them or deal with them, can be very helpful. The connection can be made through books, tapes, letters, or support groups. Whatever the mode, the connection can help normalize the experience.

EXTERNALIZE: YOU ARE NOT YOUR PROBLEM

Externalizing, a method for changing spoiled identity stories, was first developed by Michael White of Australia and David Epston of New Zealand (White & Epston, 1989/1991). They found that people and families dominated by severe problems, including schizophrenia, often internalized a new, pathological identity. They became identified with the problem and forgot the person or the family that existed before and beyond the problem. To gently remind people of themselves and their resources and identities beyond the problem, White and Epston devised a method for separating the problem from the person. They treat the problem as being outside the person's and family's true self, like an alien and unhelpful presence. Through the process of asking questions and making comments that presume this separation, they found that clients and their families eventually rediscover and reconnect with their resources and their nonproblem identities. The motto for this method is: **The person is never the problem; the problem is the problem.** Don't get them confused. Even though this was not originally presented as a step-by-step process, we have found that breaking it down into steps makes it easier to learn. Each of the eight steps is amplified here with a case history and/or sample questions.

1. *Find a name for the problem.* Use the person's or family's own words, or jointly come up with a name that really fits the problem.

I call the problem Judas, because, like Judas in the Bible, the problem is a betrayer even though it had good intentions (to lose weight), and it could end in death just like Judas ended up. The tables turned on him just like the problem (anorexia) does as it destroys your life.

2. *Personify and begin to externalize the problem.* Talk to the person or family as if the problem is another person with its own identity, will, tactics, and intentions, which often have the effect of oppressing, undermining, or dominating the person or the family.

Sample questions:

"When Paranoia whispers in your ears, do you always listen?"

"So Depression has moved in with you for the last month?"

"How long has Anorexia been lying to you?"

*Judas has lied to me for thirteen years, since right after high school. I was overweight and needed to lose some pounds, but Judas took it too far. He told me food was my enemy and that I could never lose enough weight and that this was something that I could control. He told me my self-worth was minimal and that I had nothing to offer anyone. He told me I would never be a good teacher and persuaded me not to try. As a result, he put a lot of doubt and confusion into my mind regarding my self-worth and my vocation. I know now that those were all lies because, with God's help, I have proved to him that **I can** be a good teacher and that I do have worth because I am made in God's image. Judas has pushed me around by being a dominating force in my life as I have cut myself off from my family and other people around me. He has tricked me into believing that I am not worthy of a male companion, and that I don't need my (menstrual) period for my body to function as it should. He has pushed me around by putting a lot of self-doubt in my mind and he complicates my ability to make decisions with confidence. Judas tells me that I have to always be on a schedule, and he decreases my flexibility and interest to have variety in my eating and life in general. He has planted many "seeds" of fear in my mind, which include the fear of change, telling me that I need to always keep things the same. One of the biggest lies he has told me is that I can't change and live a "normal" life and that this is the way my life is to be. He has tried to convince me that the Lord wants me to live this way in order to keep me humble, and that this suffering helps me relate to the Lord, as He knows what it means* *to suffer. When all of these things take place, along with more I have failed to recognize, I know it is Judas talking and not my real self. Despite all of his lies and tactics, I have learned the* **REAL** *truth, which is that I am made in God's image and that He has a plan and future for my life and He wants me to be well and happy. That truth, God and His word, is what sets me free.*

3. *Find out how the problem has dominated, disrupted, or undermined the person's or family's life or relationships.* How has the person felt dominated or forced by the problem to do or experience things he or she didn't like? Investigate areas of:

❖ Experience or feelings arising from the influence of the problem.

❖ Tactics or messages the problem uses to convince people of their limitations or to discourage people.

❖ Actions or habits the problem invites or encourages the person or the family to do.

❖ Speculation about the intentions of the problem in regard to the person or relationships.

❖ Preferences or differences in points of view the person has with the problem.

Sample questions:

"When has Jealousy invited you to do something you regretted later?"

"What kinds of foods does Anorexia try to get you to avoid?"

"Why do you think that Anorexia wants you to go to your grave without realizing you are dying?"

The effects of Judas on me and my family have caused a lot of grief. Seeing me "wasting away" in the early stages broke my family's hearts as they saw me deny the nutrients needed to function on a daily basis. No matter how hard they tried, they couldn't reach me. I cut myself off from them and their willingness to help me. Judas has dominated my health, as I am not functioning as a woman my age should. Even though I am at a safe weight, my body is still not functioning properly to enable me to have children if I so desired. He has also "wasted" several years of my life as my education and teaching career have been delayed due to hospitalization and time spent in counseling. Judas has decreased my productivity, as at times I have not worked to my full potential in certain areas. As far as food and nutrition goes, for years I have not been able to see and enjoy food for what it is—nourishment. Judas has made me think of it as an enemy and something to control. I have been very rigid with my eating, sticking to only the "safe foods." Even though good nutrition is important to me, he has taken it too far, as my rigidity indicates. Judas has also inhibited my interest in finding a "mate," as he has worked on my self-esteem, telling me that I am not worthy of anyone and that no one would have a desire for me. I am realizing that I have no one to blame for these thoughts but myself. I am responsible to reject what I know is not true and gear my mind to focus on the truth and use rational, logical thinking.

4. *Find moments when things went better or different in regard to the problem.* What moments of choice or success has the person had in not being dominated or forced by the problem to do or experience things he or she didn't

like? Inquire about differences the person has with the problem.

Sample questions:

"How have you stood up to the Temper Tantrum Monster?"

"Tell me about some times when you haven't believed the lies Anorexia has told you."

The last time I can remember not having the problem was when my family was still together and before my sister left home to get married and go on with her life. It was sometime before the age of eighteen. However, even in my early years of life, self-esteem was a problem, so I am not sure when the onset of this began. The symptoms have always been there. I can't remember what it is like to be "free" from this. Times when I have overcome it and not believed the lies Judas tells me are during my devotional times, during prayer, my daily walks, and basically the last eight years, as I have had a desire to beat this and maintain spiritual, mental, emotional, and physical health.

5. *Use these moments of choice or success as a gateway to alternate (hero/valued) stories of identity.* Encourage the person, or his or her intimates, to explain what kind of persons they are. What allowed them to have those moments of choice or success?

Sample questions:

"What qualities do you think you possess that give you the wherewithal to oppose Depression in that way?"

"How do you explain that you are the kind of person who would lodge such a protest against Anorexia's plans for you?"

As I look back on my journey through this part of my life, I realize that, with God's help, I am stronger than I thought, as I stand up to Judas and fight his lies. As a first step, I admitted that I needed help and sought it through outpatient therapy and then at Johns Hopkins Hospital where I was inpatient for six hard months. This was difficult, as I was away from home and had no control over my eating or my life. With God's help, I have completed my college education while dealing with Judas's lies, and I persevered and worked hard at trying to change, but deep down in my unconscious mind felt safe listening to his lies and living the way I had been conditioned to.

Another way I have stood up to Judas is to incorporate RET Theory, using rational thinking, which was very helpful and gave a great deal of insight. That was another turning point for me. Of all the times I have stood up to Judas, the most beneficial and lasting help I receive is during my devotions. The freedom I feel as I seek the Lord gives me tremendous spiritual strength and insight. It is then that I really see it as it is—a **DESTROYER.** *When I am in prayer and focusing on God and His will for my life, and when I do my journal writing, I am motivated to beat it and I can see the devastating effects Judas has on my life.*

6. *Find evidence from the person's or family's past that supports the valued story.* Who are the people from the past or present, dead or alive, who knew or know the person or the family when this problem had no influence? Can this evidence be a reminder of past accomplishments, qualities, and resourcefulness? What does the person remember about his

or her life that fits with the valued story rather than the spoiled story?

Sample questions:

"Are there people who have known you when you are not depressed who could remind you of your accomplishments and that your life is worth living?"

"What do you think your best friend would say if she could hear you talk about your small victories over self-harm?"

"What incidents from your past would help me understand how you've been able to take the extraordinary steps you've taken, despite hallucinations whispering in your ear?"

"What can you tell me about your past that would help me understand how you've been able to take these steps to stand up to Anorexia so well?"

My family are the primary people who knew me before Judas took over my life. They have told me they miss the "witty" person I used to be. My former minister, who is also a dear friend, also knew me and often reinforces my worth and potential without Judas in my life. As I journey through this battle to freedom, I plan to see myself as God sees me—in a new, more competent way, and free to enjoy the life that awaits me.

7. *Get the person or family to speculate about a future that comes out of the valued story.* What kinds of changes will result as the path of resisting the problem is continued or expanded?

Sample questions:

"As Jan continues to disbelieve the lies that delusions are telling her, how do you think that will affect her relationship to her friends?"

"How do you think that realizing you are onto the illusion of hallucinations will help you think of yourself differently?"

"As you continue to stand up to Anorexia, what do you think will be different about your future, compared to the future Anorexia had planned for you?"

As I continue to stand up to Judas and resist his lies, my future will be full of hope and happiness. I will have freedom as I focus on God's truth and learn to enjoy food in a healthy way as it should be, not used as a tool to cope. My mental, physical, and emotional health will be greatly improved as I become stronger and more productive in all areas of my life. It will be as if a "weight" has been lifted off my shoulders as I feel better about myself and am able to make decisions without the usual doubts. I will be more flexible with my eating and in my daily activities, and my rigidity will be a thing of the past. When Judas sees me standing up to him and realizes that I mean "business," he will no longer "pester" me or dominate my life. But more importantly, as I stand up to Judas, God will be glorified, as He is the reason for this new freedom, and I will be able to help someone else who is battling this "monster."

8. *Develop a social sense of the valued story.* Find a real or imagined audience for the changes you have been discussing. Enroll the person as an expert consultant on solving/defeating the problem.

Sample questions:

"What do you think John's decision to ignore the whispers of Paranoia tells you about him that you wouldn't have otherwise known?"

"Whom could you tell about your development as a member of the Anti-Diet League? Could that person help celebrate your freedom from Unreal Body Images?"

*The changes that I need to make will take time and **ACTION** on my part. No one can do it for me. I will have to take one day at a time and surrender my will to the Lord. When others see me with a new attitude about myself, food, and the role Judas has played in my life, that is when they can validate these changes I am making. My immediate family, my coworkers, and my friends are the people who will see these changes.*

SEPARATE THE PERSON FROM THE ILLNESS, AND EXAMINE THE EFFECTS OF THE ILLNESS ON THE PERSON

It is essential to find a way to reclaim the person from the illness in CSMI situations. Too often, the person has begun to be viewed, and even to view self, *as* the illness. As William Osler said, "Ask not what disease the person has, but rather what person the disease has." Typically, when a person becomes identified with or dominated by an illness, several things occur:

- ❖ *Isolation.* CSMI often invites people to withdraw from life and from other people.

- ❖ *Silence.* Having CSMI can convince a person that he or she is abnormal, weird, or different, and shouldn't speak up when uncomfortable, in pain, or ill. The person decides not to speak up for self for personal needs.

❖ *Discouragement or dire predictions for the future.* The disturbing and sometimes long-lasting nature of the CSMI can lead to the person's or other's getting or giving messages like: "You'll never get better," or "You are deteriorating."

❖ *Restrictions and narrowing of the person's activities and world.* Because of previous problems or others' discomfort, people with CSMI often avoid potentially unsafe or challenging situations, avoid going out of the bedroom, or stop getting out of bed. Therefore, they don't meet anyone new or participate in new situations, increasing the likelihood of chronicity.

❖ *Undermining of self-trust, confidence, and intuition.* Many times, clients suffering from CSMI begin to doubt their own sense of things, thereby clouding their intuition and self-confidence.

❖ *Self-devaluing and shame.* People who suffer from CSMI can become convinced they are ill because of some personal flaw or misstep. They may also feel that because pain or illness is somehow shameful or a comment on a person's basic worth, they must hide it from people.

Helping people both to challenge the idea that they *are* the illness and to get out from under the domination of the illness is crucial to improved functioning and recovery from CSMI.

SUMMARY POINTS
CHAPTER THREE

❖ Remember that there is a person beyond and outside the mental illness.

❖ Search for evidence of the person beyond the illness, and evoke both experiences of and recognition of this other, more valued, and preferred identity.

❖ One effective approach to reclaiming or creating more valued and preferred identities is externalization—a step-by-step method that systematically helps separate the person's sense of self from the illness.

❖ Help people to recognize the insidious effects of the illness on their lives, and to reclaim their lives and identities from the illness.

CHAPTER FOUR

Revaluing People's Experiences

*O*NE WAY TO THINK *about psychiatric problems is: they are reflections of devalued, invalidated aspects of a person's experience. Even if disturbances are triggered by biochemical processes, they still have psychological or emotional content. In fact, we suspect that some of the "psychotic" experiences that were seen over the years in psychiatric hospitals were posttraumatic dissociative states that were treated inappropriately—that is, they weren't taken seriously, and the people experiencing them were given the message that those experiences were bad or crazy. So labeled, these "crazy people" were often placed in contexts that further traumatized them. The devaluing messages and disturbing contexts served to further entrench the problems and increase the likelihood of additional disturbances.*

Many people with serious psychiatric problems have experienced severe and multiple traumas, if not before their first severe disturbance, then afterward. They may have been living on the street, raped or beaten, arrested by the police, and so on. If unaddressed, these traumas may show up as psychotic-like experiences or as "crazy" or self-destructive behavior.

Some of the experiences that might appear to be "crazy" may be dissociative. Or, the experiences may arise from nondissociative processes, but still could benefit from being taken seriously and validated. The first step in revaluing people is acknowledging the experience.

ACKNOWLEDGING EXPERIENCE

Jay Haley (1973) has related an experience that he had early in his career as a therapist. He was treating a psychiatric hospital patient who was constantly complaining that his stomach was filled with concrete. At a loss as to how to get the man to stop having delusions, he described the situation to his supervisor, Milton Erickson. Erickson asked whether Haley had ever tasted the hospital food. They had a good laugh about that, but after he returned to the hospital, Haley tried the food and found that his own stomach felt like it was filled with concrete. This is a relatively trivial situation compared with other things psychiatric clients might experience, but it points the way to the first idea we think goes some distance toward revaluing people's experiences.

Befriending the Devil

Bill had a woman, Karin, come to see him. She was experiencing multiple personality. During one of her sessions, a personality emerged and spoke to Bill—a devil named Astaroth. He growled, angry and threatening. Astaroth began threatening to kill Karin. Then he left about as quickly as he had come. When she returned, Karin was very upset. It seemed to her that Astaroth was a devil that had been possessing her. She wondered if perhaps we might consider an exorcism.

For a brief moment, Bill seriously considered an exorcism. Then he came to his senses and remembered that Astaroth was ultimately a part of her experience, albeit in a different and distorted form. Doing an exorcism would be like saying this part of her was no good and she had to get rid of it. She was already doing that and it wasn't helping.

So Bill started having conversations with Astaroth. Astaroth actually had a pretty good sense of humor, for a devil. He laughed at some of Bill's jokes. For example, at one point, Astaroth told Bill that it was his job to kill Karin. Bill asked him if it was a good job; that is, did he get any benefits or a good retirement plan with the job? Astaroth burst out laughing in spite of himself.

Bill also asked Astaroth about the plan to kill Karin. What was the purpose? He told Bill he must kill her to protect her. Bill was a bit confused by this logic, but persisted, gently asking questions until Astaroth told Bill that he had to kill Karin to ensure that no one else would abuse her. Bill mentioned that he had heard a quotation recently: "There's nothing as dangerous as an idea, when it's the only one you have." Astaroth seemed quiet and thoughtful after that. At the beginning of the next meeting, Astaroth was present as Karin walked in the door. He told Bill that Karin had a razor in her purse and had plans to hurt herself. He asked Bill to take the razor and throw it away. So, after a while, Astaroth and Bill developed a good relationship. During the course of the next few weeks, Astaroth turned into a little girl, who had been abused. Then, the little girl turned into Karin.

The point here is: if the therapist can respectfully approach all the experience that the client has, and can acknowledge and value it, sometimes what was troublesome becomes more "integrated" and less troubling. Astaroth, once befriended and taken seriously, became an ally in the treatment. Remember, we are referring only to the experience part of things at this point. We are not suggesting that if the client begins talking about how he has to kill his next-door neighbor, we would value that and give the message that all is OK. We would, of course, listen respectfully and nonjudgmentally, and then ensure, as much as possible, that the person did not act on this plan.

Even if the person is in the midst of a delusional, psychotic state, listen and give weight to the experience. Don't dismiss it as a mere expression of a neurological imbalance. Find a way to validate and value what is taking place, even if others view the client's perceptions as psychotic. Excerpts from a case of Tim's will illustrate this point.

Amelia had previously been hospitalized in a state psychiatric facility. She presented in a private hospital emergency room one night, appearing disoriented. The attending psychiatrist's view was that Amelia was experiencing psychotic decompensation, was paranoid and delusional. She was also described as hearing voices and as manifesting thought disorganization. Amelia's diagnosis was schizophrenia, paranoid type. The psychiatrist recommended that she be rehospitalized in the state facility, since she had no insurance. When she was told of this plan, Amelia became violent, threw things and stated that she would not go back to the place where she had been raped and abused. The psychiatrist called Tim for consultation and help with Amelia.

Tim decided that it was important not to dismiss Amelia's claims of rape and abuse as mere manifestations of her delusional state. When he asked Amelia to explain to him about the rape and abuse, she gave a fairly confusing, contradictory account of the aliens who had raped and abused her during her previous hospitalization at the state facility. Tim did his best to follow this, and then asked her if she had ever been raped or abused before her hospitalization. She hesitated and then said, slowly, "Yes," while shaking her head "No." She was calmer now, but appeared detached. She began speaking about how her paternal grandfather lived in her home while she was growing up. He had made, she said, numerous attempts to engage her in inappropriate sexual activity, but she had always found a way to block or avoid his physical advances. Her older sister, however, had not been able to avoid the abuse, and Amelia had seen them engage in sexual activities just short of full penetration. As she discussed the effect that this abuse had on her sister and on her, she became more oriented, eventually coming out of the "psychotic" state.

Tim found out that Amelia had called Child Protective Services prior to coming to the emergency room, so that her children would be cared for during her hospitalization. Tim explored how, in the midst of what appeared to be psychosis, Amelia was able to act so protectively and rationally toward her children. As they talked about her commitment to her children, she came back to reality more and more. It was finally decided, with the agreement of the psychiatrist, that she did not need to be hospitalized that night. The next morning, she collected her children from the care setting in which they had been placed. Tim was able to follow up with outpatient sessions.

SEPARATING EXPERIENCE FROM ACTION

We make a distinction between action and experience. It's OK to have experiences, even disturbing ones, as long as they do not determine one's behavior. We are trying to get clients to realize that no matter what experience or feeling they have, they can choose what to do about it. They do not have to get rid of the suicidal impulse to keep themselves from committing suicide. They do not have to get rid of the hallucinations in order to stop yelling at people when they are walking down the street.

Observers might say that this is easier said than done, but we have ways to coach people into making this separation.

We are very careful to acknowledge and value a feeling or experience, while also being careful to separate the feeling from the action. We might say, "I know right now you are feeling mad enough to hit someone. It's OK to feel that mad. And it's not OK to hit anybody." Or, "You have the sense that someone is beaming shock waves into you while you sleep. We don't know why you are having this experience, but, while we are working on this, it's important not to do anything that might get you in trouble. Going up and confronting the man who lives above you is not a good idea and may get you kicked out of your apartment."

Sometimes, it is not enough to acknowledge the experience and separate it from the actions. We must go further and actively give the person permission for whatever experience he or she might have been avoiding or devaluing.

GIVING PERMISSION

We have developed another method for revaluing experience. It involves relatively rapid resolution of posttraumatic disturbances. The method is based on a simple idea: People dissociate and devalue aspects of their experience as a result of their traumas, and these aspects begin to "have a life of their own," which can lead to inner or outer disturbances.

Writing about men who were experiencing posttraumatic psychoses and neuroses, Kardiner and Spiegel described one man who had a feeling that seemed to have a life of its own. "He had, in fact, a profound reaction to violence of any kind and could not see others being injured, hurt or threatened. . . . [However] he claimed that he felt like suddenly striking people and that he had become very pugnacious toward his family" (quoted in Herman, 1992, p. 56).

Some years ago, Jay Haley (1963) noted the similarities between psychotic and hypnotic experiences. Both can involve distortions of perceptions, depersonalization, hallucinations, and automaticity of behavior and experience. The crucial difference is that, in hypnosis, people feel OK about themselves and their experiences. In psychosis, people feel badly about themselves and their experiences.

Our approach, then, is to revalue people and their experiences. This is not just an abstract concept. We take very simple, yet powerful, steps for doing this revaluing.

1. *We examine the symptoms that people are experiencing.* Is the person hallucinating? Is he or she plagued by feelings of fear? Does he or she get enraged beyond what is called for in the situation? We begin to focus on the recurring problem that the client or his or her intimates are complaining about.

2. *We extract a statement that is in the form of a negative or positive injunction:* "You shouldn't/can't/won't" or "You have to/must/should." These are reflections of what are sometimes called negative and positive symptoms of schizophrenia. Negative symptoms refer to things that are normally present in people's experience, but are notably lacking in this person's experience, like absence of emotion or flattened affect. Positive symptoms are things that are intrusive and amplified compared with the usual experience. For example, many people hear voices in their heads at times, but in disturbing psychotic experiences, they are much louder, more intrusive, and compelling, and, congruent with our view, usually unremittingly berating.

We construe these experiences as being driven by injunctions—statements about what the person must experience or is prohibited from experiencing.

If the person has intrusive visual hallucinations, the injunction might be: "You must see and attend to these images." If the person feels fear most of the time, the injunction could be: "You have to be afraid." If the client has frequent rages, the injunction might be: "You must be angry."

3. *After we find the form of the injunction, we give permission and valuing messages to counteract this injunction.* For example, we might tell a person who has been hearing disturbing voices, "You don't have to hear voices." Or, "You can ignore the voices." If the person is dominated by fear, the permission message might be: "You don't have to be afraid." If the person is not experiencing any feelings at all, the permission message might be: "It's OK to feel."

Remember that we do not give permission for destructive actions. We would say to someone, "You can feel like you want to scream and not scream." We would never suggest, "It's OK to scream at people." We are only dealing with experience here. In our view, there are no inherently "bad" experiences; there are only those that have come to disturb the person because he, she, or someone else has judged that experience to be wrong or sick, and has decided that it must go.

USING INCLUSION

Bill heard from a former client who is now a therapist. She told him she was reading a book on borderline personality and had realized that something Bill had told her during the course of their treatment together had prevented her from becoming "borderline." "How?" Bill asked. The client lived far away from the city in which Bill practiced, and she had called one time, distressed that she was becoming too close, and therefore too vulnerable, to Bill. Bill had told her, "Well, you know that you are there and I am here. I can be as far away from you and as close to you as you need. And I can be there and here at the same time. And I can be close and distant at the same time." This, she reported had melted the inner conflict she had been experiencing.

This method, similar to the one above, also involves giving permission, but this time the permission is given in a way that includes both sides at once. "You can be hallucinating and in touch with reality at the same time." Or, "You can be frightened and calm at the same moment."

A NOTE OF CAUTION

We must stress here that we are well aware of the frightening and irrational nature of many people's experiences while they have psychiatric problems. We do not mean to minimize them or suggest that they are merely messages from their psyches that need to be analyzed and dealt with. We are suggesting that treating these experiences with respect and validation often lessens their grip on the person and shows a way out of the intrusive or debilitating experience.

SUMMARY POINTS
CHAPTER FOUR

❖ Some "psychotic" experiences may be reflections of posttraumatic symptoms.

❖ Another view of psychotic and disturbing experiences is that they may reflect devalued, invalidated aspects of experience taking on a life of their own.

❖ There are several methods of including, validating, and valuing experiences:

1. Acknowledging experience.

2. Separating experience from action.

3. Giving permission.

4. Using inclusion.

*Collaborating with Clients,
Their Families, and
Others in Their
Social Environment*

*F*AMILIES OF THE CHRONIC *and severely mentally ill are tired of getting a bad rap for causing their children's disturbances (Anderson, Reiss, & Hogarty, 1986; McFarlane, 1991). Instead of blaming families, we take a collaborative approach to treatment, which includes families in the shaping of the treatment and draws on their expertise.*

How do we go about creating a collaborative, nonblaming atmosphere in working with families? First, the expertise and knowledge that families and clients have should be given at least as much weight as the expertise of therapists. Families know a lot about what works and what doesn't work in their situation. They are also exquisitely sensitive to being blamed and dismissed by those who might help them. If we listen, they will teach us about their unique situations and guide us in finding things that work and are respectful to their lives, their struggles, and their values.

ENGAGING FAMILIES IN TREATMENT PLANNING

We regularly make families part of the treatment planning process; they are consulted about goals, directions, and responses to the process and methods of therapy. We also make ourselves and the treatment process as transparent as possible: diagnostic procedures, conclusions, and case notes are available and understandable to clients. Dictating treatment notes in their presence can be very engaging and makes it apparent that our work together is a partnership. In general, our approach to families has five characteristics.

1. *We are careful to ask questions and offer speculations in a nonauthoritarian way, giving the family ample room and permission to disagree or correct us.*

We were seeing a family and couldn't help noticing that the oldest son and the mother answered all the questions we asked. We said that, in some theories, this would be considered part of the problem. If the child acted in a parental role, the family hierarchy was confusing, making the environment ripe for problems. What did the family think about that? The father immediately spoke up and said that he sometimes felt as if he were excluded from the decision making about the daughter, who was diagnosed as manic-depressive. The son was at first adamant that he was not taking a parental role, which we accepted, but the other family members convinced him that he was indeed being parental much of the time.

We must stress that we were perfectly willing to drop the idea of hierarchy problems if the family did not agree that it was relevant or accurate. Our Socratic questioning style gave the family an opportunity to consider our concern and then make a contribution to the change.

2. *We typically give families many options and let them coach us on the next step or the right direction.* Sometimes this applies to something as simple as the time lapse between sessions: "Would you like to come back? If so, would a week be the right time or too soon to tell if what we talked about is helpful? How about two weeks or a month? What works best for your schedule?"

If we are very concerned about a person or an issue, we are forthright about it and make a recommendation for *our* preferred interval between sessions, which the family is free to accept or discuss and modify.

At other times, we give multiple-choice options for the directions for treatment or the therapy discussion: "Is what we are talking about helpful to you? Is this a good direction to be pursuing? Would you like us to talk more about the right place for your son to live, or should we be focusing more on the hallucinations?"

3. *If we have an idea and realize that we have been keeping it as a hidden agenda, we make it public and include it in the conversation—not as the truth or the right direction, but as an idea, a personal perception, or an impression.* We want to let families know that we have ideas and opinions, and some of them are informed by our professional training and experience. But we do not have the Truth or the Ten Commandments for how to live correctly or how to be mentally healthy. We don't want to have to keep our opinions to ourselves. We are certain that they leak out in our questions and nonverbals anyway, so we take care to say them in a more tentative way, giving ample room for disagreements.

Bill was working with a family in which the son was regularly violent in the home. After the family tried many solutions and directions, the violence was continuing. Bill then told a story about how his father had told him that he had learned one thing from raising eight children. Kids have to hit brick walls to learn about limits. Bill explained that his father had said that he had tried to warn each of his children when he saw that they were acting in a way that would potentially harm their futures. But it was as if the kids were riding a motorcycle toward a brick wall. Early on, before he had learned better, Bill's father had even stood in front of the brick wall, trying to shield a child from the consequences of his or her actions. After the same experience with several children, though, he had finally realized that all kids learn this way.

Was this family standing in front of the brick wall, providing soft love for their son, and would a harder kind of love, one in which he would receive consequences for being violent, be better for all concerned? The parents and, amazingly, even the son, agreed. We began to work on setting limits and providing consequences for violence (e.g., calling the police, living in another place for a time after the violence, and so on).

4. *We focus, as we wrote in an earlier chapter, on eliciting, highlighting, and using client and family strengths rather than focusing too much on the pathologies, deficits, and hidden agendas clients and families might have.* This tends to lift the family members up, rather than pull them down or make them defensive. We are also willing to confront and try to change destructive patterns of family interaction when we see them. But again, we try to do this in a way that doesn't blame anyone for having bad intentions or bad character traits. Instead, it invites the various family members to examine the undesirable effects of these interaction patterns on all or some of them.

5. *To create a collaborative climate, we focus on learning and attaining clients' and families' goals, based on their perceptions of the problem, rather than just on what we have decided they need to work on.* In the following case, the emphasis is on eliciting the cooperation of parents to facilitate positive change for their "disturbed" or out-of-control offspring. The collaborative family therapy helped a delusional young man make the transition to independent living.

A young man, Turner, was admitted to the state inpatient psychiatric hospital because he had delusional beliefs. He would tell people that he was a rock-and-roll singer, a player for a major league baseball team, the mayor, and so on. He had

*stopped eating and was not having bowel movements.
Turner's behavior was described as "psychotic in nature." He
had had various problems for eight years. He had quit school
and joined the Army, but left the service after only one year,
claiming it was not for him.*

*Turner returned to his former high school, but was kicked
out for physically assaulting a teacher and a student. He was
able to get various jobs, but he quit and moved on after several weeks. He was unable to maintain an ongoing intimate
relationship, preferring to move in with girlfriend after girl-
friend for short periods of time. He had experimented and
used various drugs, including mescaline, Quaaludes, PCP,
LSD, hashish, and marijuana. At the time of admission,
Turner was living with his parents, Camille and Brice.
Turner's two siblings were living away from home and en-
joying successful careers.*

*It was not really necessary for Turner to work to support
himself. Someone in the family—usually Camille, but secretly
Brice, who worked two jobs, or the grandparents—would give
him money when he was broke. He had "maid service" from
Camille, could "come and go" from the house whenever he
wanted, slept most of the day, and went carousing at night.
Camille would also drive him wherever he wanted to go. In
general, Camille felt that Brice was too tough, and Brice felt
that Camille was too easy.*

*One of the major problems in the case was keeping Turner
in the room with his parents during therapy. Any time he did
not like what was being discussed, he would get angry and
leave. Brice and/or Camille would go after him. He would
eventually return, only to leave again.*

*After numerous attempts to keep him in the room failed,
Tim decided to work mainly with the parents. Tim suggested
to them that if they wanted Turner to be different, they should*

surround him with an atmosphere of movement and change. When they were asked how long it had been since they had gone out as a couple, they indicated it had been a long time. As such, a "date" would be a change that Turner would observe. Camille's getting out of the house and spending time with people her own age would be another change. Perhaps they could rearrange all the furniture in the house, buy a new style of clothes, travel to new places, and so on. In addition, Brice and Camille could act "as if" they had a normal son and do the things they would do if he did not have problems. If they acted like normal parents, maybe Turner would act in an age-appropriate manner. They were asked to keep all of this work private so that it could have the intended impact on Turner.

As Brice and Camille followed through with recommendations along these lines, Turner "spontaneously" began to reorganize and change his own life. This process rapidly accelerated after Camille, with the support of Brice, purchased a small business and was no longer at home most of the day to meet Turner's every need. Turner followed this lead and, shortly thereafter, engaged in an activity appropriate to his age range—a steady job. Tim stopped seeing them several months later, after these changes stabilized.

CONJOINT VS. INDIVIDUAL THERAPY WITH CSMI

How do we decide when to see a family and when we will work individually? Several factors influence this decision. One is: How involved are family members in the person's situation? The more involved parents, siblings, or extended family are, the more likely we are to involve them in treatment, because they will have valuable information and input into the treatment process. In addition, they will be impacted by whatever happens in treatment, and they might have become part of the pattern that is supporting the disturbance. We are not implying here that they have caused the problem or have some stake in keeping their family member's disturbance going. People make adjustments, and those adjustments sometimes unwittingly support the disturbance. A family that lets the anorexic child throw tantrums when they keep certain foods in the house has adjusted to the disorder in an unhelpful way. A mother who tolerates her adult child's hitting her and calling her names because he has a psychiatric problem has adjusted in a way that supports the problem.

Tim's next case illustrates exactly this point.

A Dangerous Situation

Bart, a well-built 16-year-old, was admitted to the child and adolescent unit of the state inpatient psychiatric facility. He was both verbally and physically abusive to all members of his family. He had punched his mother, Luella, and had threatened to kill his father, Abbot. He exposed himself to his mother and had made sexual overtures toward her. Bart's history of serious problems dated back to his childhood, when he had been diagnosed and treated for "hyperactivity, petit mal seizures, and enuresis." As a student, he had a history of extensive academic and behavior problems.

Abbot and Luella separated shortly before the hospitalization, and Abbot began dating other women. Bart and his father had become hostile to one another, and Bart, who lived with his mother, had become extremely disrespectful toward Luella's authority. There had apparently been a history of spouse and child abuse by Abbot.

Bart improved dramatically in the hospital after he was taken off all medications prescribed by his community pediatrician. His hospitalization spanned six weeks. Abbot was a reluctant participant during inpatient treatment, and refused to continue in family therapy after Bart's discharge from the hospital.

Outpatient therapy was arranged for Luella and Bart. During the first session, Bart made fun of his mother, called her names, and commented on how stupid she was. All attempts to block such behavior and to define her as in charge of him were extremely ineffective; if anything, these endeavors made matters worse.

After seeing them together, I met with Luella alone, to assess her situation. It was much worse than I had imagined. She described Abbot as a tyrant who physically and psychologically abused her. She related that he had beaten and sexually abused her during most of their marriage. Luella said that Abbot would not allow her to have friends or to go out of town. She considered keeping our appointment a milestone because she had never driven as far as the mental health clinic on her own. In order to arrive successfully, Luella had practiced the route several times prior to her appointment.

In addition, Luella told me that Abbot never gave her sufficient money to properly manage the house. After hearing this, I was somewhat astonished when she stated that she still loved Abbot and wanted him back. She even considered that she possibly deserved his treatment. Luella had little confidence and doubted if she really had the ability to go back to school or to get a job.

After meeting with her, I met with Bart; he did his best to aggravate me. He called me names, took my phone apart, and threw paper airplanes at me.

At the next session, I met individually with Luella. I told her that if the parent(s) lead the way for change and resolve their problems first, the child is more likely to change. Or, if the parents can solve their problems, they might simultaneously help their offspring change. When I recommended that I help her reorganize her life, as well as help her with Bart, she agreed. I spent approximately 75% of the time at subsequent appointments seeing her individually. She agreed to keep our work private and tell no one. This would help derail Bart's ability to plan his counter moves. It would also give her more time to resolve her problems and reorganize her life as a single parent and as a woman. My hope was that, as Luella changed, she would set the appropriate example for what she wanted Bart to do. Surrounding him with an atmosphere of change, which he could not easily identify, would make it easier and more likely to spark subsequent changes within him.

Along these lines, I encouraged Luella to make friends, get out of the house more frequently, check on returning to school (with a plan to leave various educational brochures around the house), seek employment, and so on. Since she had a history of threatening to call juvenile services and the police, and not following through, I instructed her to actually follow through on such actions when Bart was out of control. Luella initially found this very difficult to do, but gradually accepted both the short- and long-term benefits. Bart began to appreciate Luella more, and his behavior improved after several visits from legal authorities.

In school, Bart was more of a problem after discharge from the psychiatric facility than previously. He was placed in a special class for students with emotional problems. He hated being in that class and was extremely disruptive. He directly challenged the authority of the teachers, and, on more than one occasion, left the teacher's aide in tears. He refused to complete assignments as directed, aggravated other students, and frequently missed school.

I attended several school conferences with Luella, and we did our best to keep him in a normal academic setting. Luella thought that, if Bart passed, he might do much better the next year because he wanted to attend a vocational-technical program at the school. She explained that he was good in carpentry, auto mechanics, and other skills requiring the use of his hands. The school system recognized Luella's efforts, as well as her support of them, and gave Bart more leniency than his behavior warranted. He barely passed; but, with much persuasion on the part of a pupil services worker, the school system reluctantly gave Bart an opportunity to attend the vocational-technical program.

No one expected Bart to survive in a normal school setting more than a month. He proved everyone wrong and was not an academic or behavior problem thereafter. His grades improved dramatically, and he received mostly As and Bs during his junior and senior years. Attendance problems also ceased.

Over time, Luella made friends, took college courses, obtained employment, survived her divorce, and began to date. As planned, the more she reorganized and restructured her life, the more Bart improved.

Follow-Up

Two years later (six years from the only psychiatric hospitalization discharge date), a follow-up was done. Bart was working as a machinist in an industrial plant. No major problems were reported in any area of his life, and he had recently married.

Luella had relocated to another area and was reportedly doing well. Bart's relationship with Abbot, who had remarried, continued to be less than satisfying. Abbot did not make ongoing overtures to spend time with Bart and/or to show an interest in his life.

WORKING COLLABORATIVELY WITH OTHERS

Our methods for developing and maintaining collaborative relationships are important because others are both affected by and affect the problem in the client's context. Working individually sometimes brings about only temporary change. Working with families can have a good effect. Working to change other parts of the social context may also be required.

When working with others, we use the following principles:

❖ We look for possibilities to highlight progress and solutions.

❖ We collaborate by asking the views of others and speaking about our views only as views, not as truths.

❖ We do not attribute bad motives or unchangeability to others.

❖ We attempt to change our own and others' views and behavior until we find something that works.

What happens when the treatment professionals disagree among themselves on a case? Our best advice is to keep the conversation going. You never know when an unexpected opportunity for cooperation may emerge. At least the other professionals will be dealing with the real you rather than an imagined image conveyed by others. In the following case, things went wrong initially between Bill and the other professional involved. Later, things became more cooperative.

Bill began seeing a woman, Dolores, who was having religious delusions. She would become convinced that any move she made would have eternal consequences. If she made the right move, she would dwell eternally in heaven with God; but if she acted wrongly, she would forever be condemned to the fires of hell. Most of the time, she was lucid enough to realize this was nonsense, but when she was delusional, this dilemma seemed deadly serious. She was seeing a psychiatrist, Dr. Burns, in whose view the matter was purely biochemical. As long as she stayed on her medication, all would be well. All was not well. Even though she was quite committed and precise about taking her medicine, she still had the delusions at times, although they were a bit diminished in intensity.

Dolores decided to seek psychotherapy for the delusions and began to work with Bill. When Dr. Burns heard about this, he went ballistic. Why was she wasting her time and money on such foolishness when her problem was biochemical? Talk therapy could do nothing for her delusions. Furthermore, Dr. Burns knew of Bill, and he told her that Bill did "paradoxical therapy," which could be very dangerous. (Bill had taught a workshop on that subject some ten years before, but no longer used the technique.) Psychotherapy was an unscientific technique, he told her. Only biochemical approaches were based on science.

Dolores left that session with Dr. Burns very frightened. That night, she began to have delusions. Was Bill the devil? Was Dr. Burns the devil? What was the right move? She called Bill, who was traveling, and tracked him down in a hotel in which he was teaching a workshop. Bill returned her call during the break, and they discussed the matter. Bill told her that he understood what a dilemma this placed her in, and if she needed to, she could stop coming to see him. He also told her that he would be willing to speak to Dr. Burns, to possibly clear up some of the misunderstandings between them. She mentioned that she had suggested that to Dr. Burns, but he had refused.

As they talked further, Dolores calmed down and decided that she did not have to decide right away which was the best move. She would come for another session with Bill, then decide whether she wanted to continue.

Bill decided, with Dolores's permission, to write a letter to Dr. Burns. First, he explained that he no longer did paradoxical therapy, and he understood the concern that Dr. Burns might have with the use of that method. Bill included some material from a paper he had written, criticizing the overuse of paradox.

Next, he acknowledged that Dr. Burns had a legitimate right to be skeptical about whether "talk therapy" could make a difference in Dolores's symptoms, but a true scientific approach would be to do the experiment and then examine the results, rather than make a premature conclusion. How about giving Bill and Dolores several months to find out whether this approach had a beneficial effect?

Bill received no reply from Dr. Burns, but he heard from Dolores that he had grudgingly accepted the situation, saying he would take a "wait and see" attitude.

Dolores began to improve. We found that some of her symptoms were related to her abuse within a religious setting, and did some revaluing work (see Chapter 4) with the delusions. Dr. Burns was genuinely impressed. He had known the course of Dolores's symptoms long enough to notice that going several months without delusions was very significant. Dr. Burns never contacted Bill or offered any direct appreciation of the work he did, but he referred to Bill several of his patients over the next few years, and they exchanged polite correspondence regarding these cases.

Another case from Tim illustrates how to creatively use a case conference (a meeting with other professionals to discuss the problem situation) to facilitate change with a chronic geriatric client.

Reamer the Beamer

A geriatric woman had spent most of her adult life in an older state mental hospital, then was transferred to a new state inpatient psychiatric facility, and was later living in the community in supervised housing. After being released, she did well, and psychotropic medication was discontinued. Yet, from the time of placement in the community, she regularly conversed with "Reamer," who "beamed" her messages from above. Some time later, she refused to see a doctor for recurring pain in her back, and she was not bathing regularly. She told the staff that "Reamer" had told her not to see anyone except a chiropractor. In fact, she was not to make any decisions without first consulting Reamer.

Her case arose during a regularly scheduled conference for those in the housing project, and I suggested that the staff simply channel their concerns and suggestions through "Reamer the Beamer." The group found my recommendation amusing and challenged me to try it first. Although it was not my original intention (I had never met the woman), I agreed.

When she entered the room, I greeted her, told her who I was, and asked her if I could examine the area of discomfort in her back. She agreed. Afterward, I thanked her for her cooperation and told her to sit down. Next, I told her that I had received and was still receiving from the rest of the group a theme or a beam. (Each time I used the word beam or "Reamer," I looked up.) I explained our concern about her health and my feeling that "Reamer" would agree with the idea of her seeing an advanced chiropractor—a neurologist. In addition, I thought "Reamer" would agree that it would be embarrassing for a woman her age to be bathed by others, and that "Reamer" would accept her solving the problem herself.

Several weeks after that encounter, I learned that she was diagnosed as having osteoarthritis and was doing quite well taking aspirin. In addition, her personal hygiene had improved.

At the initial follow-up (almost five years after discharge from the state hospital), the woman was residing in a nursing home with no major problems. Two years later (almost seven years after her hospital discharge date), she continued to do quite well.

Tim relates a case in which he enlisted the help of someone in the client's context.

Gladys, a middle-aged, single woman (who had an extensive history of psychiatric hospitalization), was discharged from the state inpatient psychiatric hospital to the supervised housing project. After her discharge, she had problems dealing with staff and other residents. When upset, Gladys became verbally abusive and, at times, physically assaultive.

One afternoon at the clinic, the receptionist told me that my appointment was early. Gladys was terrorizing the clinic— talking in a loud, vulgar, rapid manner (and what she was saying did not make much sense). The receptionist also indicated that Gladys wanted to hug everyone, and people were afraid of her.

When Gladys saw me coming toward her, she ran away, laughing, and went into the women's bathroom. I sat patiently, waiting for her to come out. When she did, I pointed my finger at her and said, "Come with me." Fortunately, she cooperated and followed me into my office.

I told Gladys to sit and to talk as rapidly as needed, as loud as needed, with as much vulgarity as needed, for as long as needed. As she proceeded, I repeatedly interspersed various words whenever she stopped to take a quick breath. The typical words I used were **comfort, peace, relaxation, calm, rest.** Within fifteen minutes, Gladys was calm and relaxed and began to tell me what was bothering her. She explained that she really cared about other people and wanted to be nice to everyone, but people took advantage of her kindness. She said that she could not sleep at night because one of her roommates stayed up too late, and she really needed a good night's rest.

Gladys indicated that others did not understand her, and she really wanted people to like her. She talked about her confusing interactions with other residents in the home, as well as with her family, and how sad she was over the recent death of her grandmother. After she had stated the major issues bothering her, I asked Gladys to listen as I talked. I started by indicating that she had had a very confusing and difficult life, that she was a good woman who wanted affection, and that others probably did not understand her very well. After this, I told her that I would help her now and in the future, but for the moment she most needed a good rest.

I then went back to using the words **comfort, peace, relaxation,** and so on, and indicated that, at "home," she could sleep and rest as comfortably that evening and thereafter as she was resting right now. I repeated this suggestion several times. I then told Gladys to rest for as long as she needed, and said I was leaving. I said I would return in about an hour to talk with her if she desired. When I returned, we had a normal conversation, and I agreed to see her again that week.

Gladys rested much better that evening and did not have any major problems until the next day. She then began *behaving as she had the day before. I visited Gladys at the psychosocial center, and the residential director for the supervised housing project agreed to attend. I repeated the procedure from the day before, as the residential director watched. Again, Gladys responded well to the calming approach.*

After the session, I met with the residential director and asked her to use this approach with Gladys in the home if there were problems at night. She agreed and had her first opportunity that evening. She was successful in helping Gladys to calm down and get some sleep.

SUMMARY POINTS
CHAPTER FIVE

❖ Families with CSMI members have too often been unfairly blamed for their children's problems.

❖ Working collaboratively with families involves making changes in family interactions without blaming anyone. These ways of working can help both the CSMI person and the other family members.

❖ Sometimes, working with parents is the best way to help their out-of-control offspring. Doing so does not mean that the parents are to blame for the offspring's problems.

❖ Family interactions may be unwittingly supporting or allowing problems of a family member.

❖ If a collaborative relationship is not created with other professionals, friends, families, and roommates, treatment may suffer and relapse is more likely.

❖ Look for opportunities to highlight progress and solutions involving others in clients' lives.

❖ Ask the views of others, and speak about your view as views, not as truths.

❖ Do not attribute bad motives or unchangeability to others.

❖ Keep the conversation with others going in a respectful way until a way to cooperate emerges.

CHAPTER
SIX

*Creating a New
Vision of the Future*

*O*NE OF THE BIGGEST *stressors among people with chronic and severe psychiatric problems—and their families—is a sense that the future holds the same horrors as the past. These clients and their families lose their hopes and dreams for the future. In this chapter, we detail ways to rehabilitate a realistic vision of the future and get clients and families moving toward creating that future. We call it the Victor Frankl Strategy after a story Victor Frankl tells about one of his bleakest moments and how he came through it.*

Frankl was a psychiatrist in Vienna just prior to World War II. Because he was Jewish, he was arrested and sent to a death camp by the Nazis. He was later transferred to several different camps and came close to death on many occasions. One day, he and some other prisoners were being marched through a field in the middle of winter. They were being taken to a work detail some distance from the camp. Frankl was ill with a respiratory ailment. He began coughing and found that he just couldn't stop. He tried to keep walking, but finally collapsed to his knees, racked with the cough. A guard came over and began beating him with a club, telling him that they would leave him there to die unless he got up and kept walking. Frankl did not want to die, but he wasn't able to get up and walk. At that moment, he found that he was no longer in the field in Poland; instead, he was vividly imagining himself in Vienna again. The war was over and he had been liberated from the camp. He was giving a lecture on "The Psychology of Death Camps," in which he not only detailed the horrors of the Nazi pogrom against the Jews and others, but also gave his ideas about how people psychologically survive such horrors (mainly, that they have meaning and purpose, the basis for his lo-gotherapy approach). During his lecture, he recounted the day he almost died in the snowy field outside the death camp in Poland. He talked about his inability to get up and walk, and then, amazingly, he found the strength to stand up and move his feet. As he was recounting this in his imagined lecture, in the field in Poland, his body responded to his imagined future by getting up and walking. He kept himself involved in his imagined lecture throughout the walk, the work detail, and the return trip to the death camp. Finally, collapsing into his bed at the death camp that night, he fin-ished the lecture in his mind and got a standing ovation from his imagined audience. He had never given such a bril-liant talk as the one he had imagined.

In 1990, Bill saw Victor Frankl tell that story in Anaheim, California. Frankl had not only survived that day in Poland, but ultimately survived the death camp experience and became a well-known writer and lecturer. In Anaheim, he received a standing ovation from 7,000 people! He had cre-ated the future he had imagined. Such is the power of a fu-ture with meaning. It can pull us forward, out of the terrible present and into a better life.

The therapist's job with clients and families who have been discouraged by CSMI is to rehabilitate for them a sense of a future with possibilities. The intent is to instill not a false sense of optimism but a realistic sense of a future that can be more satisfying than the worst moments in the pre-sent and the past—a future with meaning and purpose; a Victor Frankl future. In our experience, most of the clients and families we work with have the seeds of such visions, missions, and purposes within them. We must help them both to recognize and to make real those future visions.

THERAPY GOALS

One of the small ways to orient toward the future is to ask clients and families what they envision as the results that therapy will provide for them. Mental health consumers' groups and newsletters are filled with stories of frustrated clients and families who had a sense they were never consulted about what they wanted from the treatment process. Being asked what they want to have happen, and having their concept of the future taken seriously are empowering for many CSMI clients. We ask clients questions like these:

❖ What are the first signs that will indicate we are making progress toward the goal(s)?

❖ What will indicate that what you have been concerned about is no longer a problem?

❖ What will your life be like when you are over your difficulties?

Sometimes, getting people to be specific, even about emotional states and inner experience, is helpful. Because it is easy to misunderstand how important these goals are, we ask people to describe them in action terms, using what we call videotalk. We ask questions like:

❖ If we could see a videotape of Jim when he is being "more cooperative," what would we see him doing? What would he be saying, and how might you imagine he would be feeling in that future scene?

❖ If we could watch a videotape of you being less paranoid, what kinds of things would you be doing differently than when you are more paranoid? Whom would you believe and trust? What new things would you start doing?

If description and actions aren't appropriate or don't fit, we sometimes ask people to indicate where they are currently on a scale:

❖ On a scale of 1 to 100, with 1 being the most chaotic and difficult, and 100 being everything going well, where have you been recently and where would you like to be that is realistically attainable?

Interestingly, just getting people to talk about and focus on where they want to be, rather than on the painful past, often makes them feel better—even before they've made any behavioral changes. Such a teleological approach fosters the "future determining the present" and is an equally valid orientation to the typical view that "the past determines the future."

INDIVIDUAL DREAMS AND VISIONS

Most people have some vision of what they'd like their life to be about and where they'd like to be in the future. But because of the psychiatric problems, for many CSMI clients, the dreams have been forgotten or put aside. Part of our work is to help restore dreams and get people moving in the direction of their life goals.

A client of Bill wanted to learn more about astronomy. He had been severely hampered by his psychiatric problem, but he still had dreams. His parents were afraid that he was setting himself up for a fall. He had tried to take an astronomy course some years before and had failed to complete it, which led to his becoming very depressed. When we discussed it, he reminded his parents that he had been taking five courses at the time, and he had not been on medications. He felt that if he audited a course on astronomy now and limited himself to that one course, he had a chance to complete it. His parents consented, under the condition that he would not define himself as a failure if he had to drop out. He agreed.

Often, when people are suicidal, they have lost touch with their dreams and have forgotten that the future still has possibilities.

Spray Painting a Workable Future

Bill was seeing a family in which the 15-year-old boy was using drugs, failing in school, and getting into legal trouble through gang activities. He had been getting good grades until the past year, when he failed all his high school classes. When Bill asked him why he had failed, he professed to "hate" school. Bill asked him which classes he hated the most and which he hated the least. He hated English the most, he said, and Art the least. Why did he hate Art the least? He told me that it was because he was the graffiti guy for the gang and was good at drawing and painting. He had still failed Art (he didn't like the sculpture and mobile parts of the class study, so he hadn't finished all his projects), but he had done well in the painting and drawing parts of the class. Did he ever have any interest in earning a living doing art? I asked. Yes, he replied. How does one make a living with art? I asked. Well, one way is to paint murals, he knew. How do you get into that? I asked. Well, there is a guy in his neighborhood who paints them and takes on apprentices. But you have to have passing grades and stay in school in order to be his apprentice.

FAMILY DREAMS AND VISIONS

We also investigate what shared dreams the family has. What kind of family life do they envision and hope for in the future? We encourage families not to give up on their dreams. Who knows what kind of medical advances and therapeutic innovations the future may bring? At the same time, we help them adjust their dreams and hopes to make them more attainable, given the current conditions. A colleague of ours in Sweden told us about a family that came to therapy hoping that their daughter's schizophrenia could be cured by the innovative therapy method he was using. It took several weeks of discussion and work to revise those expectations. Our colleague knew that they were making progress when the family reported triumphantly, at one meeting, that their daughter had gone to the toilet on her own several times that week. As long as the client or the family is making progress in the direction of their dreams, they can keep their hope alive.

CHALLENGING HOPELESSNESS

Some of the people we have seen have saddened us when they narrated the negative and discouraging messages they have gotten from other professionals. We challenge hopeless and dream-killing pronouncements and prognoses that families or individuals may have heard from others. Nobody knows what the course of any psychiatric disorder will be, or what breakthroughs may happen in the future. While we were writing this book, we happened to see a television program on Christopher Reeve, the actor who was paralyzed in a riding accident. He is absolutely convinced that he will walk again, despite the fact that it is currently impossible for someone with such a severe spinal cord injury to ever walk. As viewers wondered whether Reeve is a hopeless optimist who will inevitably be let down, the scene changed to an interview with a researcher who has been developing a treatment that has made paralyzed mice walk. He showed the mice with spinal cord injuries, unable to move their legs. Next, the mice that had been given his injections were shown starting to move their formerly paralyzed legs. The researcher predicts that, within seven years, there could be a treatment available that would help Reeve regain movement.

We have recommended that people read the stories of others who have had success at dealing with psychiatric problems. There are many inspiring stories that can both validate clients and families and give some sense of hope. If none is available or especially appealing, we might suggest reading something inspiring from another area in which someone has overcome some seriously debilitating or challenging condition—the stories of "exceptional" cancer survivors or of people like Victor Frankl.

To make "impossible dreams" into real possibilities, someone must make a plan to overcome the very real barriers to those dreams. This book is filled with our suggestions and methods for overcoming the barriers faced by our clients and the families that care for them.

SUMMARY POINTS
CHAPTER SIX

❖ Many families and individuals affected by severe psychiatric problems have lost touch with their dreams and hopes.

❖ Therapy can help remind people of the possibilities of the future.

❖ It is important to challenge false hopes while keeping a sense of real possibilities and dreams alive. One way to do this is to focus on what is attainable in the near and foreseeable future, keeping open the possibility that the future may bring unforeseen breakthroughs.

❖ Detail barriers to realizing dreams, and make plans to overcome or dissolve those barriers.

❖ Challenge hopeless or dream-killing pronouncements and prognoses that families or individuals may have heard from others.

CHAPTER SEVEN

Handling Dangerous and Violent Situations

*O*NE OF THE MOST *worrisome aspects of severe and chronic psychiatric problems is the possibility that the person who is suffering from the problem may die. Suicide is an all-too-common end for these clients. Being the recipient of violence and acting violently toward others is another common occurrence. Our approach, while including traditional treatment methods such as hospitalization, also uses the family and community resources, as well as the internal resources of the person, to prevent such dangerous situations from occurring or recurring.*

One of the methods we use derives from the work of Haley (1980) and Madanes (1981). It is called a "suicide watch." We like this method because it involves keeping the client out of the hospital, using social and family resources, and making allies of family members. We think that it can even radically reduce the risk of lawsuits regarding the handling of suicidal crises, since the families are involved both in planning the suicide watch and in carrying out the treatment plan.

Tim's work with Stillman illustrates a method of involving the family to help a client who was suicidal.

Implementing a Suicide Watch

Stillman, a young, separated father of two children, was readmitted to the state inpatient psychiatric hospital after attempting to kill himself for the second time. He had been hospitalized several months previously for the same reason. Prior to this admission, Stillman was living with his parents,

Rhea and Tate, and his children were residing with their mother. The couple had a history of separations, and Stillman returned to his parents during these times.

I met Stillman and his parents for the first time at the end of the second hospitalization. At that transitional therapy session, the inpatient therapist recommended a suicide watch. Rhea and Tate were not to leave Stillman out of their sight at any time. If necessary, they were to remain no farther than arm's length away from him. That also meant that Stillman could not go anyplace without his parents or drive alone, or sleep alone; they took turns watching him through the night. Rhea and Tate were not eager to do all of this, but after acknowledging that this dangerous situation warranted such a radical approach, they agreed to keep all the conditions of the suicide watch.

Stillman was not pleased with this plan, but Rhea and Tate stuck together and stated that he could not live with them without these precautions. The plan was set for the first week at home and was to be renegotiated at the first session in the community. If the parents had any concerns about Stillman's safety before then, they were to immediately put into operation all facets of the originally proposed suicide watch. Stillman reluctantly agreed to this plan and was released from the hospital.

During the first outpatient session, all agreed that there had been no significant suicidal actions or even strong suicidal impulses. Stillman even thanked Rhea and Tate for putting forth so much effort to help him. Much of this first session was devoted to specifying behavioral changes each person had noticed prior to the previous suicidal attempts, so we could design a relapse warning and prevention plan. A list was made, and copies were given to all present. Rhea and Tate stated that they would set aside a specified time each evening to sit down and discuss any behavior(s) from the list that were beginning to surface again. Anyone could call the meeting.

Stillman cooperated with this planning process. Rhea and Tate then stated explicitly that they wanted to continue with the same version of the suicide watch as during the previous week. They told Stillman that they thought he was much improved from the time he went into the hospital, but they did not want to make an error, given the seriousness of the situation. He accepted their request without argument.

At the end of the session, I met individually with Stillman to discuss his separation and children. He did not want to talk about the separation, but was eager to share information about his children. Stillman was very fond of them and related how much he missed seeing them now and during the hospitalization. He said that he looked forward to spending more time with them. I asked him to tell me, with more and more detail, about them and how much he loved them. I also asked him if they loved him in a similar way, and he stated that the love was reciprocal.

With the preceding as a foundation, I suddenly and harshly reprimanded Stillman for lacking sincerity. How could he love his children if he were dead? What right did he have to deprive them of a father, and how would they understand his suicide, since they were children? Would they grow up thinking it was their fault? If Stillman truly loved them, should he not solve his problems and stay alive? Was it not his responsibility to ensure, to the best of his ability, that they had a secure development and a bright future? This did not require that he live with their mother, but it did require quality time with appropriate affection and guidance until they were adults.

Hearing this, Stillman sat motionless for several minutes, deeply in thought. I sat patiently waiting for him to verbally respond. When Stillman did talk, he said, "I never thought about what it would do to my children." I then told him that it was my opinion that he did not need to die as a body—only his present lifestyle needed to rapidly cease so that a new lifestyle could be born for him and his children. What kind of future did he envision for himself and his kids? We went on to plan how to reach such a future.

ELEMENTS OF A SUICIDE WATCH

❖ Only use a suicide watch when the client's family or friends are available and willing to participate.

❖ Explain the procedure to the family or friends, and stress the seriousness of the situation and their duty to their loved one.

❖ The person who has been suicidal must not be alone at any time, even to go to the bathroom.

❖ The watch must go on twenty-four hours a day, so shifts of several people must be scheduled in advance.

❖ A backup plan should be prepared, in case a watcher becomes unavailable unexpectedly.

❖ The watch is called off only with the agreement of all the parties: the family members or friends, the client, *and* the therapist.

Throughout the book, we have stressed the importance of being collaborative. In situations in which there is a likelihood of physical danger, however, the therapist must sometimes be more authoritarian, in order to ensure safety. Tim's treatment of Violet shows this different approach with a suicidal client.

Violet, a 22-year-old, was admitted to the state inpatient psychiatric hospital as a result of "severe depression, suicidal thoughts and suicidal attempts." Prior to the hospitalization, her relationship with her 52-year-old boyfriend, Egan, had deteriorated, and her grandmother (and namesake), with whom she was very close, had just died. Violet was also abusing drugs and alcohol, and she had quit her job. Her family ostracized her after she began living with Egan; he was her older sister's former husband, and her parents, especially her father, detested him. Leah and Emil (her parents) described Egan as having been too friendly with Violet from the time she was 13 years old.

After Violet's sister and Egan separated, his overtures to Violet increased. Leah and Emil were aware of this, constantly lectured Violet to stay away from him, and tried to forbid her from seeing him. Yet, Violet moved out of their home and eventually moved in with Egan. Egan drank excessively, which they felt contributed to Violet's drug and alcohol abuse.

After two months in the hospital, Violet was discharged during the week between Christmas and New Year's.

The situation rapidly deteriorated after Violet began seeing Egan again. He told her how much he cared about her, but he simultaneously was involved with another woman. Violet's interactions with him left her in a state of confusion. Subsequently, she shot a rifle in the direction of her own head, and later took a combination of thorazine, aspirin, and several pain killers. Her friend Sandra, with whom she was living, contacted the former inpatient therapist, and Violet was rushed to the emergency room of a local hospital and was subsequently admitted to the intensive care unit.

After sufficient improvement in her physical condition, Violet was readmitted to the state psychiatric hospital. She responded to treatment, concerns about "suicide and severe

*depression" diminished, and she was converted from invol-
untary status to voluntary status. Although Violet showed
significant improvement, the hospital staff was concerned
about another relapse once she returned to the community,
since very little in her life had changed.*

*Violet was still in love with and chasing Egan, who really
did not want her. Violet did not have a job or an active lead
on one. She had few friends and few positive activities. In addition, Violet often disagreed with her inpatient treatment
and frequently returned from passes in an inebriated or
drug-induced state. She functioned quite well, however, much
of the time she was in the hospital.*

*The inpatient therapist had been able to engage Leah in
treatment, and there was a vast improvement in their relationship. He had also established a positive relationship with
Sandra. Upon discharge, Violet would be living with Sandra
and her family, and this community linkage was significant.
Sandra was caring, supportive, and willing to extend herself to
help her troubled friend.*

*Active aftercare planning was under way, but certainly not
finalized, when Violet submitted a written request for a 72-
hour discharge. The hospital was in a bind. Her case managers
felt Violet needed longer treatment, but knew she would not
meet criteria to be recertified and returned to involuntary status. Therefore, Violet's request was honored, but against medical advice.*

*I was very familiar with this case and had talked with Vio-
let on several occasions. When the inpatient therapist informed
me of her decision, we took immediate action to organize as
thorough an aftercare plan as possible.*

*If I could find a way to reconnect her with Emil (her father),
I hoped that would cushion the loss of Egan and simultaneously
begin to resolve the father–daughter problems. I wanted to invite Leah, Emil, and Sandra to a transitional therapy session.*

Violet objected to Emil being involved, but said that it was OK to invite her mother and her friend.

I was not satisfied with Violet's stance and went to the hospital to meet with her. I wanted her permission to contact Emil and invite him. After much persuasion, Violet reluctantly agreed. I subsequently called Emil and told him that I wanted him to attend a meeting at the hospital. He gave me many excuses as to why he could not attend. I responded that, given what had taken place the last time his daughter left the hospital, she could be dead within two weeks.

I explained that there needed to be more significant changes and more social stability in her life immediately. I let him know that I did not think that Violet could tolerate being rejected by both him and Egan, and that improving her relationship with him would be a much better option than helping her get along with the man he hated. Emil still would not consent, saying he needed time to think about it. We set up the transitional therapy session not knowing whether Emil would be present. Fortunately, Emil came. Violet was astonished. She had assured me Emil would never change his mind.

At that session, there was a cooperative effort by all present to help Violet make more appropriate plans to reorganize her life in the community. Sandra told her that she would help her come up with a daily schedule until she could get another job. Leah and Emil told her that she was welcome in their home anytime. Violet had not been "home" in a long time, and this was a very significant gesture on the part of her parents.

Other plans were topped off by an invitation from Emil for Violet to attend dinner on Sunday. At the end of the session, I invited all present to the next session, to be held in the community, but Violet objected. She stated that she would only agree to have Sandra attend. I disagreed and told Violet that if she wanted to work with me, I would be in charge of the therapy. Concerned about her suicide risk, I explained that I considered her situation to be one of the most serious that I had ever been involved with, and I would be unwilling to take any chances.

Initially, this led to a power struggle, but eventually we compromised. As long as Violet was improving, she could decide who came to the therapy sessions. If I was concerned about her in the least way, I would have the option of meeting with any person(s) I deemed appropriate. I also made it clear that improvement would not be judged solely on our two perspectives; I would intermittently contact those present to ascertain their opinions. This compromise was supported by the other participants, and Violet finally consented.

I met with Violet and Sandra on several occasions in the community, and Violet steadily improved. After several sessions, Violet requested that I only meet with her, and I agreed. I had been verifying over the phone that she was improving. I discovered that her relationship with Leah and Emil was gradually improving, and Violet was considering a more active search for employment. No one was concerned about her being suicidal. So, we jointly decided to stop treatment and keep the door open if any further needs developed.

Follow-Up

At the initial follow-up, Violet told me that she was working full-time and had a new boyfriend. Over a year later, I ran into Emil, who told me how happy he was with her. He said that Violet had taught him how to drive and had also taken him and Leah to visit relatives who lived out of town. I asked him how Violet was doing with the new boyfriend. He smiled and told me that she was now married, the mother of a little boy, and working full-time.

At the last follow-up (almost eight years from the psychiatric hospitalization discharge date), Violet continued to do

well. Her marriage was stable, her son was healthy and grow-
ing, she was still working full-time, and she was about to be-
come a Sunday school teacher.

She now had a most positive relationship and connection
with her family. She and her siblings would gather at her par-
ents' home several times a month to visit.

In cases like this, we think it is essential to have an external "reality check" (in Violet's situation, her parents and
her friend, Sandra). Too often, clients, if seriously suicidal,
might tell us that everything is improving and be secretly
planning to kill themselves.

DEALING WITH VIOLENCE

Another case of Tim's shows the way we deal with violence.

An adolescent, Page, was admitted to the child and adolescent
unit of the state inpatient psychiatric hospital after threaten-
ing the members of her family with a knife and tearing the
house apart. She had done this kind of thing on numerous
previous occasions.

Page was the youngest child in a household consisting of
her mother, Rachel, and two older sisters. The older of the two
sisters in residence had a two-year-old son. A younger sister
had been placed in a group home because Rachel had been
unable to control the girl's behavior. An older brother had
moved out of the house. Page's parents were divorced, and her
father was no longer involved with the family.

The inpatient therapist indicated that there had been no
episodes of violence while Page was in the hospital. She also
related that Rachel had told her that Page's violent behavior
had always stopped once the police arrived at her home.

When the police would bring Page to the emergency room for psychiatric evaluation, her mother was somewhat embarrassed because Page sat quietly while waiting to be seen. Prior to this hospitalization, she had always been sent home.

At the time of discharge from the psychiatric facility, Rachel was requested to make explicit her expectations of Page for the first week at home, as well as the consequences Page would face if she did not cooperate (Haley, 1980; Madanes, 1981). At the end of the session, Rachel was asked whether any adult relatives or friends lived nearby and could help her, if necessary. She said her sister, Wilda, lived next door, and an older male neighbor, Abner, might also be available. Rachel was asked to bring them, as well as the two older daughters who were living in the home, to the first outpatient session.

At that session, after everyone had gathered, I immediately stood up and asked Page to walk toward me. I told her to lie face-down on the floor. She seemed stunned by this, but cooperated. I then instructed the others to get down on the floor too, and hold Page's legs and arms tightly. Everyone was carefully coached on how to do this as a team. Special emphasis was placed on not applying any pressure or weight on the trunk and head areas. Rachel was to coordinate all of this and ensure that Page was restrained, but not hurt. She agreed to this role. I wanted to establish a context of safety for Page and ensure that Mom was in charge of the family.

After practicing how to approach Page, get her to the floor without injury, and restrain her, all the participants were asked to return to their chairs. I then asked Page if she remembered the "code green team" in the hospital. She did remember, so I explained to the others that this team would come running to the scene when someone was acting in an out-of-control manner. I made an analogy between this and calling the police in the community. I then stated matter-of-

factly that Rachel could be in charge of such a team at home, and avoid the embarrassment of repeatedly calling the police and going to the emergency room.

Page, as well as the others present, found this perspective rather novel and all agreed with the idea of having a code pink team and a code red team. Code pink would be a show of force that would be a preliminary to code red, which required actual physical restraint. If Page responded to code pink and did as Rachel expected, she would not be restrained on the floor. Rachel agreed.

Rachel called to cancel the next two sessions; she could not arrange transportation with any family or friends, and could not afford a taxi. Because she expressed a genuine interest in continuing, I arranged to do a home visit. Their home had four very small rooms: a kitchen, television room, and two bedrooms. The two older sisters shared a room with the two-year-old, and Rachel and Page slept together. There were no doors for privacy, and curtains were used as partitions. The bathroom was in the bedroom where Rachel and Page slept. There was literally no extra space and no way a person could have privacy. Although very crowded, the apartment was very neat.

During the initial home visits, I met with the family, as well as Wilda and Abner, and rehearsed once again what would be done if there was a problem. The violent out-of-control behavior ceased after two episodes in which Page was actually restrained. This behavior was never again an issue in the therapy. After several sessions with no problems, I recommended that, because things were going so well, we should take a break from therapy. All the participants agreed.

About two months later, I received a call at home from Rachel. She said she had been rather depressed for several weeks. To make matters worse, she was now having trouble getting Page to attend school. Rachel stated that maybe she *(herself) needed to be admitted for psychiatric help. I talked on the phone with her, at length, and then arranged a home visit for the next day. She agreed to arrange for everyone to be out of the house so we could have privacy.*

At that visit, I told her it was my opinion that she was having problems because she had done so well in helping Page. In a very practical way, Rachel was becoming more and more unemployed as a mother, as her daughter did well. This made sense to her. I then proceeded to explain to her that her "depression" was a metaphor for a dying lifestyle, and, as such, it was appropriate to mourn, as long as it did not last too long.

To solve the problem, Rachel would need to develop a new lifestyle and reorganize her life to be more complex. She would need to think of herself as not only a mother, but also as a woman. Rachel would also need to consider training or a job because her income (welfare) would decrease by half when the next oldest daughter in the home turned 18, in about a year. In four years, when Page turned 18, she would have no income. Rachel responded with enthusiasm to these ideas. She was asked at the end of the session to have her daughter and her girlfriends present at the next meeting.

To deal with the school attendance problem, Rachel and Page were transported to the school for a meeting with the guidance counselor and vice principal. Page talked about how the other students were making fun of her, and how that made it hard for her to come to school. The school agreed to help Page learn to handle other students who were making fun of her. It was arranged for Page to meet briefly with the guidance counselor on a daily basis until the problem was resolved.

At the next home visit, I asked the daughters to help Rachel develop more of a life on her own. They were not in charge of the rules or regulations of the house, but were to help their mother initiate a new lifestyle. They readily agreed, and I asked each of them to think of one idea along these lines. One daughter suggested bingo, one suggested going out with a girl-friend in the evening, and one suggested a movie. Rachel had to do what they recommended or come up with a better idea, and she was to bring something back from each place she went. One of her girlfriends, also present, agreed to help implement and monitor the plan.

Rachel followed through, repeating the procedure for several weeks. There were no major problems individually or in the family after this. During an initial follow-up with Rachel, she was about to begin a training program, told me she had moved to a bigger house with more room, and announced that one of her older daughters was getting married. She also indicated that Page was still difficult to manage at times, but she could now handle her.

Follow-Up

At the last follow-up (seven and a half years from the inpatient discharge date), I learned that much had transpired in Page's life during the intervening years. She had quit school, married at age 16, and had two children. The marriage had deteriorated, and she was now in the process of divorce. The earlier problems in her marriage and the need to adjust to the separation had been upsetting to her. During both crises, she had engaged in brief outpatient treatment to regain her balance.

In talks with Page and Rachel, both agreed that Page was still easily provoked, but they also confirmed that there had been no recurrence of violence since the days of the restraining technique. In discussing these earlier times, Page defined herself as a "brat." Page and her mother now had a positive relationship. Rachel occasionally baby-sat with her grandchildren.

SUMMARY POINTS
CHAPTER SEVEN

❖ Dangerous (suicidal and violent) behavior is all too common among persons with severe and persistent psychiatric problems.

❖ In situations where physical danger is possible or likely (suicidal and violent behavior), the therapist must sometimes take charge of the therapy to ensure safety.

❖ A suicide watch is a method for involving family and friends in a twenty-four-hour vigil to prevent hospitalization and keep the suicidal client out of harm's way.

❖ An approach that enlists family and community supports, both for "reality checks" and as resources, can be effective in diminishing or eliminating dangerous behaviors and preventing future hospitalizations.

CHAPTER EIGHT

Effective and
Respectful Treatment of
"Borderline" Clients

*W*E COULDN'T CONSIDER THIS *book complete without dealing with the issue of "borderlines," the ubiquitous diagnosis of the 1980s and 1990s. We are both veterans as therapists, and we remember the days before there was such a diagnosis. We are a bit disturbed by this label, which now appears to be quite common. It seems to us that it is often used to connote a client who is frustrating to psychiatric facilities and treatment personnel. Or is it a shorthand for someone whom the staff or a particular psychiatrist or therapist finds troublesome or unlikable? Or a catchall for clients who don't neatly fit into another diagnostic category and seem unresponsive to treatment?*

Because it is ubiquitous, we thought we'd better address it. We have some ideas about what works with these clients.

DEFINING BORDERLINE

First, we want to give a down-and-dirty sense of the kinds of clients *we* are referring to when we say borderline. A popular book on the subject of borderline personality disorder captures the essence of the problem in its title: *I Hate You—Don't Leave Me* (Kreisman & Straus, 1991). People with this diagnosis are usually ambivalent about treatment. The *DSM-IV* (American Psychiatric Association, 1994) says that they are unstable and fear abandonment. They often feel compelled by suicidal or self-harming intentions and behavior, and often express intense anger toward those who are treating them or toward friends.

113

Bill saw a client who had been to see a psychologist and had been "fired" by him. She reported that when she had told the psychologist that she was suicidal (which she had been for years), he had insisted that she make a contract with him agreeing not to attempt suicide. If she felt she couldn't stop herself, she must agree to call him and go into the hospital. She told him that she did not feel comfortable with such a contract and would prefer not to make one. She needed an escape hatch in case her suffering became too much, and making that contract would feel to her as if she had no possible escape. He insisted that she make the contract, for legal and ethical reasons. She finally complied, but instantly became compulsively suicidal. It was all she could do to manage her compulsion to kill herself. When she returned for the next session, she told him that she could not work with him, given his insistence on the contract. Following that conversation, he wrote her a certified letter in which he recommended that she enter a psychiatric hospital for her safety. She saw the letter as an attempt by him to cover himself legally, not as a statement of concern for her, and it left her even more despondent.

When she came to see Bill, she mentioned the incident with the previous therapist. Bill asked her how she was doing, now that she had her escape hatch back. She said that she was feeling much less suicidal, even though she thought about killing herself regularly. Bill asked her how many years she had been seriously thinking about killing herself. Over twenty years now, she said. Had she ever made an attempt? he asked. No, she replied. Would it be better to work without such a contract then, and trust her to handle the suicidal impulses as she had for the twenty-some years? he asked. She said that it would in fact help her to manage the suicidal impulses if she didn't have to have such a contract. Bill said that he usually made such a contract with suicidal clients, but, given her unusual circumstances and response to such contracts, he would be willing to work with her without a contract, and she would be responsible for her suicidal impulses. She reported at the next session that her suicidal thoughts and impulses had diminished markedly since the previous session.

STAYING FLEXIBLE

This case underscores the initial point we want to make about treating borderline clients: the key is *flexibility.* One size never fits all in psychotherapy, and that is especially true in working with these challenging clients.

We think that borderline features are sometimes evoked or exacerbated by "resistant therapists," that is, therapists who are inflexible and punitive in their response when these clients do not respond as they "should" to standard approaches.

Bill was seeing a client, Jennifer, who would regularly regress during sessions; she would curl into a fetal position and stop talking. When asked questions, she would respond in a small, child like voice. One day, Jennifer was talking about how upset she was that she procrastinated and did not handle paperwork in either her personal or professional life. She was concerned that, even though she was quite good at her job, she would be discovered as incompetent at work, because of her lack of attention to the detailed paperwork that accompanied her job. She began to go into her regressed, fetal state as she talked about this. Bill began telling Jennifer about how bad he was at doing paperwork. He told her that his wife had been threatening to buy tables and desks with A-frame tops, so Bill could not pile any papers on top of them. He also told her of his chronic problem of not returning phone calls in a timely manner, about which he was very embarrassed, and which occasionally created real problems with other people in his life. Jennifer immediately sat up and came out of the regressed state. The session continued. At the next session, Bill mentioned that he had noticed how, when he told Jennifer about his paperwork and phone call problems, she had improved. Why had that happened? She said that usually Bill told stories about things that he or other people did in which they struggled with a problem but somehow resolved it. This story about himself had no such "happy ending," and it had made her feel better about herself. She had always felt like a "bad patient" before. Perhaps she, like the people in the stories, was expected to improve, and because she wasn't improving, Bill would eventually tire of her and dismiss her from treatment. Hearing that Bill (whom she perceived as a "together" therapist) had problems had made her feel more normal and had taken the pressure off.

VALIDATING CLIENTS' EXPERIENCE

Another factor that increases clients' difficulties with a therapist is not validating clients' experience. This is challenging for most therapists; they fear that validating a client's experience is tantamount to giving permission for acting out or self-harm. But we make a clear distinction between validating experience and encouraging actions.

Bill was on a teaching trip and was asked to consult with a client, Marianne, who had been diagnosed borderline personality disorder and was perceived as one of the most difficult patients at the hospital where Bill was teaching. Marianne agreed to the interview with this unknown visiting expert, but when the time approached, she became scared and suspicious and vowed that she would not speak during the interview. Bill asked her what had brought her into treatment and she replied quickly and almost imperceptibly that she had been severely depressed since she was eight years old (she was in her late twenties at the time of the interview). She said that nothing had ever helped and when she was given antidepressant medications, she would immediately swallow the entire bottle in an attempt to end her miserable life. She had never succeeded in her suicide attempts, much to her regret, she said. Bill told Marianne that he was surprised, given her description of her situation, that she would agree to the interview with him. Why did she? She replied without hesitation, and in a stronger voice, that she was willing to do anything that might help. Bill told her he suspected that most people didn't really see that or believe that about her, but it seemed clear to him. Then Bill told her that he had seen a story on television about a young woman with a chronic degenerative illness who had fought a legal battle for the right to kill herself. When she was interviewed by Mike Wallace of the news program 60 Minutes, *he asked her why she wanted to kill herself. She replied that she didn't really want to die, but she certainly did not want to live a life that was as miserable as the one she was leading. Mr. Wallace pushed her again on the issue: Why did she want to kill herself? She again reiterated that it wasn't dying that she was interested in, but in ending her suffering. Bill asked Marianne if that resonated with her experience. She sat up and said that she had never been able to say it, but that was true for her. She did not really want to die, she only wanted not to be so miserable. She actually wanted to live. The staff at the hospital was surprised to hear her say this; they had all been convinced that she was dedicated to dying.*

Next, Bill noticed cigarette burn marks on Marianne's wrist and some more burn marks peeking out from under her long-sleeved sweatshirt. When he asked about them, Marianne said that she regularly burned herself. What was that about? Bill asked. It was to distract herself from her emotional/psychological pain, she told him. Bill then told a story he had heard from Bruno Bettelheim at a conference. As part of his training, Bettelheim had been in analysis in Vienna many years ago, and had often shared the waiting room of his analyst with a 10-year-old schizophrenic boy. In those days, strict rules prohibited patients from talking to one another (it might contaminate the treatment), but Bettelheim was hard pressed to stay silent when the boy would routinely wander over to the window box and pull small buds off the cactus plant and chew on them. The boy's mouth would bleed as his tongue and lips were cut by the cactus spines. Finally, after enduring these horrific scenes for over a year, Bettelheim confronted the boy and asked him to stop this outrageous behavior. The boy looked up calmly and told him that, compared to his psychic pain, chewing the cactus was actually a relief. Marianne listened to this story with great interest and again said that most people could never understand, but it was true for her also.

From that point on, the interview became much more interactive. Marianne talked more and offered some surprising information about a recent breakthrough she had had. Her newest medication was working, unlike all the previous ones she had taken. She was not only experiencing less depression, but had even experienced moments of joy for the first time in her memory. She had not taken an overdose of these medications, and had some small hope that the future might be better.

Notice that until Marianne felt validated in her misery, hopelessness, and suffering, she seemed uncooperative and "resistant." Once she felt understood, she spontaneously offered some solution-oriented reports and expressed some hope. If you do not embrace the dark, you will rarely get to the light with these clients.

GIVING PERMISSION—WITH LIMITS

We revisit some material from Chapter Four here. As part of validating experience with borderline clients, it seems very important to give permission for their ambivalent or discouraging emotions and their impulses (again, not their actions). So, it would be important to give clients permission to feel suicidal (along with the opposite possibility of not having to feel suicidal), but one must be careful, when giving this permission, that clients are not invalidated nor given a sense that their other feelings are not right. Permission to act on the suicidal feeling is not given. It would be appropriate to give clients permission to feel as if they will never get better, but inappropriate to give them permission to stop therapy or stop going to work. The important tasks here are: (a) separate the feelings, thoughts, sensations, and other internal experiences from actions, and (b) give lots of permission and validation for the experience, but clear messages of limits and boundaries for action.

With borderline clients, validating and giving permission for hopelessness, pain, suffering, and despair seem especially crucial, but these are difficult emotions and thoughts for therapists (who tend to be an optimistic bunch) to validate.

Another crucial area for validation is ambivalence. If we were to use this approach with the client in the book we mentioned above *(I Hate You—Don't Leave Me),* we might communicate something like: "It's OK to hate me. And you can be afraid of me leaving you. You don't have to be afraid of me abandoning you. And it's OK to feel afraid of that. You can hate me and not hate me at the same time, even if that doesn't make any logical sense."

If the client talks about being too vulnerable, the permission could be: "You can feel vulnerable and safe, exposed and protected, at the same time."

WORKING WITH BORDERLINES

We offer four principles for working effectively and respectfully with borderline clients:

1. *Be flexible.* Don't stick with your standard procedures. Observe the results of your words and interventions, and then make adjustments to personalize your approach.

2. *Give permission and validation* for inner experience, including ambivalence, discouragement, anger, hopelessness, and so on.

3. *Set clear behavioral limits,* without being punitive. The best way to do this is to be collaborative. Be transparent, and speak your concerns about the behavior and your intentions in setting the limits.

4. *Hang in there.* Don't get hooked into the crisis of the moment or the client's sense of hopelessness. As with other chronic and severe clients, part of the healing effect is staying connected to the client through times when other people are likely to give up on or blame the client.

Another crucial feature of treating borderline clients is to gently but firmly set and hold behavioral limits in the therapeutic relationship. One must be especially careful not to be punitive in this respect. Many therapists get angry or exasperated with these clients, and the limits they set are inconsistent or punitive. Think of your responsibility as a kind of good parenting. Limits and consequences are not set to punish children, but to inculcate responsibility and to develop an ability to think ahead and anticipate consequences. But the best parents do all this with empathy and kindness.

One way to set limits is to engage the client in a collaborative discussion. This involves stepping out of an authoritarian role as the therapist who knows what's best for the client, and into a more egalitarian and transparent relationship.

Bill was consulted by a client who wanted to check out three therapists to whom she had been referred, to determine which one she would see. She explained that she had just come out of a psychiatric hospital where she had been committed after making harassing phone calls to a college counselor at the college she attended. She had developed an obsession with this counselor and had begun to call him at the counseling center twenty or more times each day. She would never speak, just get him on the phone, hear his voice, and hang up. After receiving a number of such nuisance calls, the counselor got them traced and discovered who was making the calls. He talked to her and told her that she should stop or he would have to take legal action. She persisted and he spoke to her again, asking her to stop the calls. She was warned by the phone company that she would be charged with a crime if she continued, but continue she did. After a time, the counseling center stopped taking direct calls for the counselor, but this client obtained his unlisted home number and began the same obsessive calling. He changed to a new unlisted number, but somehow she obtained that one also, and the calls continued. She was finally arrested, but offered the alternative of voluntary commitment to the psychiatric hospital rather than jail time. She asked Bill what he would do if she began the same phone-calling behavior with him. He said that he would call the police immediately. She asked how he would know it was she, and he replied that none of his other clients called like that, so she would be the logical suspect. She nodded and sat silently for some time. Finally, the session was over and she got up and left, never to return. One hopes she didn't find a therapist who became the unwitting target of such harassment by answering incorrectly.

As permissive as we are of any experiential disturbance, we are careful to be clear and firm on the behavioral limits.

A client of Tim's, Jan, had been cruising the bars and looking for "Mr. Goodbar"—a man who would take her home for the evening. She often landed in dangerous circumstances and had been raped once during these encounters. After Tim discussed his concerns with Jan and asked her to stop this behavior, she told him she felt compelled by "dangerous men" and didn't think she could stop. When she was sitting in Tim's office, she could quite reasonably see that she did not want to continue this pattern, but when she was alone or out at the bar, she felt unable to contain herself. Tim asked if Jan would be willing to call him, any time of the day or night, if she felt in danger of going home with one of these dangerous men. The contract wouldn't last forever, just until she could break the pattern. She agreed, and several weeks later, Tim received a late-night phone call from her. She was flirting with a man and it looked as if she were likely to go home with him that night. Tim talked to Jan and reminded her of their therapy goals, which included developing healthier relationships, and helped her formulate an excuse to give the man in order to quietly leave the bar. She was able to leave the bar alone. In the next therapy session, they built on this change to continue to help Jan move away from the old destructive patterns and into healthier relationships. Some months later, via the Internet, Jan met a man from a distant city and began a relationship with him. However, when the man came to town and, after several dates, they were about to have intercourse, he announced that he had a sexually transmitted disease, and that he hadn't wanted to tell her for fear she wouldn't have sex with him. She got angry at this deceit and asked him to leave. She broke off the relationship with the man. She was clearly making progress in breaking her old destructive patterns.

The key to the success of this intervention is its collaborative, nonpunitive nature. If Tim had become authoritarian and laid down the law, Jan would likely have rebelled at his limits. If he had become upset when she continually sought out dangerous men, she would have felt shamed and, one suspects, even more compelled.

Summary Points
Chapter Eight

❖ Beware of seeing "borderlines" everywhere. Be careful of "theory countertransference," in which therapists become enamored of their theories or labels and start to impose them on their clients or to cocreate the diagnosis with clients.

❖ It is crucial to validate and give permission for the inner experience of borderline clients (especially for their ambivalence, discouragement, and anger), while gently and compassionately setting limits for the expression of this inner turmoil.

❖ Be flexible and collaborative. Do not assume that borderline clients are not trying to get better or are aiming their behavior intentionally to get at others (including the therapist). Engage the client in a collaborative relationship that aims to find out how to validate the client and help him or her get a handle on destructive actions. Observe carefully what works and what doesn't in the course of therapy, and make adjustments accordingly.

CHAPTER NINE

Relapse Recovery and Relapse Prevention

*T*HIS CHAPTER DETAILS WAYS to work with relapses *and relapse prevention. The emphasis is on identifying and highlighting resources clients and families have used and could use to recover from and prevent relapses. It's important to anticipate relapse without predicting that it is inevitable or creating an expectation for it.*

WARNING SIGNS

One way to prevent relapse is to carefully study previous problems and glean from them warning signs that another problem could be developing. This is often done in substance abuse situations. Some of the warning signs are observable, and those should be shared among family members and other treatment and support people. Some signs, however, are internal. Only the person who is experiencing them will be aware of them.

Bill was working with a young man who had experienced severe obsessive episodes in the past. He would become obsessed that he had touched something in the incorrect way and would have to redo it until he did it right, which would sometimes entail repeating the behavior for hours, preventing him from doing anything else in his day. He would sometimes try to get out of the shower, but would accidentally brush against the shower curtain in the "wrong" way and have to get back in and clean himself all over again. He would often have to repeat the shower fifteen or twenty times and would be shivering in the cold water for the last several showers.

He knew when one of these episodes was about to happen because he felt a fullness in his sinuses and would become tense in his neck and shoulders. We agreed that when he felt these warning signs, he would immediately make an appointment with his psychiatrist to discuss the matter and adjust his medications. Just having the plan helped him feel less anxious about the possibility of another "bad" episode, but it actually worked to diminish the length and severity of the next episode.

RECOVERY PLANS

Sometimes, the best laid prevention plans fail or are not put into practice. Therefore, it is important in some cases to map out a recovery plan. This can usually be gleaned from asking about what happened as the person regains equilibrium after the previous psychiatric crisis. We usually emphasize, for obvious reasons, things that the client is able and willing to do. If the client says that the last time the delusions subsided, she was just feeling more centered, this would not be as helpful as a description of what she did when she started to feel more centered. Perhaps she recontacted friends, began going out of her house more, or started going to church services. Is there any part of those activities she could imagine getting herself to deliberately do the next time she finds herself having delusions? What could help remind her of those things?

Bill had a client who had experienced multiple episodes of severe depression. She was quite surprised when one of the first questions that Bill asked her was: "What usually happens as you begin to emerge from one of your depressive episodes?"

She thought about it and began to describe how she would start calling friends, going outside her apartment, and getting the paper to look for a job. She would also congratulate herself for having done any little thing that she hadn't been doing during the time she was depressed. She would tell herself, "You went for a walk today. Good for you!" Since she was currently in the midst of a depressive episode, Bill suggested that each day she make a list of any small things she had done that she could give herself credit for, even brushing her teeth, and go over the list each night, congratulating herself. She agreed and was able to recover from this depression much faster than usual.

One of Tim's cases shows the use of relapse and recovery from multiple recurrences of problems for a young man.

Lang, a teenager, was admitted to the child and adolescent unit of the state inpatient psychiatric facility after his parents separated and he moved with his mother to a new area. He was described as "depressed." Before his hospitalization, his mother, Delilah, had been hospitalized for the same reason.

After several months of inpatient treatment, Lang began attending the public school while still in the hospital. Eventually, he was discharged from the hospital to live with Delilah and continue in school. He was not referred to me until after he was discharged. Not long after his return to the community, I received a call from the school indicating that Lang was having problems. I made a school visit and found that the administrators were furious with the hospital for sending them this adolescent. They associated me with the hospital and, as such, I decided to let them be as critical as they wanted for as long as they wanted, without any rebuttal or defense. I was concerned that the school was possibly "getting even" with the hospital and that Lang would be caught in the middle. If Lang failed to do well in school, it would appear that his placement there was inappropriate and the school would be correct.

After they voiced their complaints, I sided with the school. In many ways, their anger was justified. They felt that there should have been a school conference before Lang came to their school. They stated that a representative from the hospital should have visited the school, explained the situation, and given them recommendations on how to deal with him. They said they had no records from the hospital, did not know his diagnosis, and so on.

Delilah was present during much of this. I asked her if she would be willing to sign a release for the school to get the hospital records. She agreed, and this seemed to appease the school. We then proceeded with the official agenda for the conference. Lang, who was rather talented musically and had a good singing voice, was singing in the halls as well as in some of his classes. Some of the older boys in the school were even getting him to sing for them while they made fun of him and called him "Stinky." The school was small, and most of the students knew Lang had been in a psychiatric hospital. They labeled him and his behavior as "crazy."

At the end of the conference, I requested the help of the principal and guidance counselor, and they agreed to keep me informed of Lang's school progress. I was also given permission to visit the school as frequently as necessary. In return, I indicated I would make special arrangements to see Delilah and Lang that week.

When I met with Lang and his mother, I strongly reprimanded Lang for being loyal to the school's image of him and told him he seriously had a strong need to reinforce the school's perspective. He could be even more dedicated to fulfilling that image by singing more in the wrong places at the wrong time, getting kicked out of school, and returning to *the hospital. (I knew he disliked being in the hospital and did not want to return.)*

After this Lang was told to act like "Stinky" in my office while Delilah and I made fun of him, as the students did. He detested the idea of practicing voluntarily what he was doing spontaneously in school. I pretended to be angry with him for not cooperating, and told him I had some more disgusting ideas if the problem continued. Delilah was instructed to continue urging Lang to act like "Stinky" at home.

Behaving like this might seem cruel, but I knew Lang was on the verge of getting kicked out of school. This behavior had to be discontinued rapidly. The intervention was successful. In addition, Lang was encouraged to continue singing, but in the right places and at the right time—in chorus practice or when alone. He did well the rest of that school year, until Delilah foolishly went to his high school prom with a student. She then became the joke of the school, and many students teased Lang about his mother.

Not long after, I received a call from the principal, stating that Lang was again in trouble. He was using abusive and foul language in school. The principal understood the predicament the boy was in and had talked with him about it, but the problem continued.

I visited Lang at home that day, after school. We went for a walk and talked. I explained that I had a better way for him not only to protect his mother's image, but even improve it. My way would require him to be more mature than most people his age. He could tell no one about it, not even Delilah. It was also a way for him to get even with those who were now making fun of him and his mother. I deliberately withheld telling him what the idea was until I felt he was sufficiently motivated and eager to hear it. I then told him that if he used all of his resources, he could exceed the expectations of not only the other students, but also many of the teachers.

Most people expected him to crumble under the pressure of all the harassment, and, in many ways, he was cooperating with their perception of getting into trouble. We discussed many ways he could outmaneuver those giving him a rough time. Subsequently, they would be frustrated instead of him, and he would be left with a sense of self-appreciation and acceptance.

We discussed the length of various phases in a person's life, and I pointed out that adolescence was really a rather short time in his total existence. If Lang prepared himself academically, he could outshine, as an adult, many of those now harassing him. He could prepare his revenge by doing well in the long run and showing up the other students, who might look good now, but might not do so well in the next phases of their lives. We jointly decided that he could work on developing his voice or doing well in sports as well as improving his grades, so he could increase his long-term chances of success.

For Lang, this was an economical and practical no-lose situation. He did not have many friends, so he could start on this project right away. He would have a constructive secret plan for now and the future. It would make Delilah look good in the eyes of the school and community, because they would probably give her some of the credit. It would also make her proud of Lang and give her some happiness. In addition, maybe she could learn from his example and do better herself. In short, it would be good for both him and his mother, now and in the future.

Lang was able to make it through the rest of the school year, and his grades improved during the next academic year. He had no major problems socially or academically the following year. No school visits were necessary, and school officials were quite pleased with his progress.

Given Lang's progress during the second year at the high school, the case became inactive. At that time, Delilah was dating, and talking about a possible marriage. Nine months later,

I reactivated the case after Delilah and Lang temporarily moved into a shelter for abused women. Delilah had married, and her husband had become physically abusive of her and psychologically abusive of Lang. Delilah decided to move from the shelter into a new community, meaning Lang would have to attend a new school in the middle of the academic year.

Delilah was taking legal action to recover their clothes; her husband would not allow her access to their belongings. This became a major problem for the now tall Lang; he had to start in a new school with shabby, donated clothes that were much too short. Additionally, his self-confidence was at a low ebb, in response to an abusive stepfather and the general disarray of his life.

Lang entered the new school in a weak and vulnerable position. Immediately, some of his peers seized the opportunity to attack a "weakened prey," and the scenario played out two years earlier immediately repeated itself. The situation led Lang to revert to previous behaviors. At the behest of his male peers, he engaged in ridiculous acts, hoping to achieve acceptance. As before, his behavior made matters worse, and he was quickly ostracized.

On one occasion, I visited the school and observed the cruel treatment Lang was receiving. Students called him names, provoked him to inappropriate behavior, shoved him, and refused to sit by him in the cafeteria. Despite this pressure, Lang tried his best to be accepted and even improved his grades. Yet, he became a social outcast. The more teachers and counselors tried to protect him, the more the students harassed him.

Something had to change in Lang's educational setting. The situation grew increasingly out of control and became the focus of attention for too many people. At a school conference, it was decided that Lang should attend an alternative school for the remainder of the academic year. Delilah consented, even though Lang objected, and he completed the year without incident.

By midsummer, another crisis ensued. Delilah began living with a new boyfriend, who was not fond of Lang or his relationship with his mother. (I later learned he also physically abused Lang.) He gave Delilah an ultimatum: him or Lang. She chose her future husband. Needless to say, Lang became distraught precipitating Delilah's call to the mental health clinic requesting an emergency appointment. One of my colleagues saw him (I was not working), and found Lang to be "anxious, upset, and tearful," but not in need of psychiatric hospitalization—despite Delilah's clear preference. Lang was being kicked out of the boyfriend's residence.

My colleague helped Lang regain his composure, and arranged for Lang to stay overnight in a Structured Shelter Care facility for adolescents experiencing behavior and substance abuse problems. The next day, we agreed he could stay there until a more appropriate setting could be found.

Unfortunately, no resource in the community would accept a 17-year-old male. Compounding the problem, Lang found his mother's rejection quite intolerable. She contributed to the problem by giving him mixed messages. She visited frequently, telling him how much she loved him, then refused his pleas to live with her. After Delilah's visits, Lang frequently received calls from her boyfriend, who reprimanded him for "upsetting her."

After a month in the shelter, with no feasible placement in sight, pressure from the facility staff was mounting for Lang to leave. Serious problems between him and his peers were not helpful to anyone. Rejection from multiple sources took its toll, and Lang was rehospitalized. Lang stayed for six months (until he was 18). He was then eligible for the supported housing component of the psychosocial rehabilitation program. He began sharing an apartment with two other residents.

To his credit, Lang was determined to graduate from high school. The Board of Education, in response to Lang's request, established an incremental plan for him to attend half-day sessions, both at the alternative school and the high school. If successful, Lang would then have the option of starting his senior year at the regular school. All went well. Lang returned to the school where he had been previously ostracized, and he graduated with straight A's. The staff of the residential program became his surrogate family and were instrumental in facilitating Lang's success.

During Lang's year-and-a-half effort to complete his education, the residential staff and I worked closely as a therapeutic team to assist Lang in ensuring that he did not relapse. We helped him to identify the signs that would indicate a return to the position he had been in several times before. He said that when he started to feel scared with others, he would begin acting in a way that he thought would amuse them and thereby win them over. He agreed to watch for the signs, as would the residential staff and I. If any of us saw the signs, we would immediately begin implementing the prevention plans.

Here is part of Lang's list of relapse prevention plans:

1. Talk to my counselor when I am getting scared.

2. Redouble my efforts to do things I'm good at when I am scared, not make myself look funny.

3. When I am feeling rejected, I will go for a run and think it over before I do anything rash.

We also made a recovery plan based on what Lang and I had learned from his several hospitalizations. We hoped he would never need it, but it made both of us feel better just having a plan in place. This involved getting a stable and safe place to live, getting reinvolved with some sort of academic or occupational training program, and getting physically active again.

At the one-year follow-up (three and a half years from his last release from hospitalization), Lang had completed nine months of supported employment, and had begun a nonsupported job. He still lived in rehabilitation housing, but the staff thought he could move into his own apartment soon. The staff appropriately emphasized Lang's move to independent living and encouraged his interest in dating.

During the next five years of this twelve-year case (I had intermittent levels of involvement), Lang made some major strides. He maintained steady employment, moved into his own apartment, was able to get his driver's license, and bought a car.

After moving out of the rehabilitation housing, he requested that I work with him again. Lang also requested the input of the community support component of the psychosocial rehabilitation program. They worked with him in cocreating what they defined as a Personal Future Plan. This entails visiting consumers in their homes or at their work sites to do job coaching or budgeting, or to offer emotional support. There have been no further psychiatric hospitalizations in over eight years.

Summary Points
Chapter Nine

❖ It's important to anticipate relapse without predicting that it is inevitable or creating an expectation for it.

❖ Part of preventing a relapse is to ensure that all concerned have a list of warning signals indicating that previous problems are about to reoccur.

❖ School and home visits can be very helpful in preventing relapse.

❖ Engaging friends, family, and other social supports can be important in preventing or bouncing back from relapse.

❖ Focus on what the person and others have done to help recovery or prevention in past experiences.

CHAPTER TEN

*General Principles for
Working with Chronic and
Severe Mental Illness*

*T*HROUGHOUT THIS BOOK, WE *have offered specific principles and ideas that we have found helpful in working with CSMI clients and their families. Here, we revisit and restate some of these ideas as general principles.*

GENERAL PRINCIPLES

1. *Don't get hooked by the hopelessness of the situation.* Decline the invitation to be overwhelmed by anxiety, urgency, frustration, and overresponsibility. Remember to breathe and take your time.

2. *For the moment, discard diagnoses and relate to your client.* No therapist has ever helped a diagnostic category. Therapists only help people. Observe and then give close attention to what works and what doesn't work with this person and family.

3. *Beware of others' evaluations.* Keep your head clear of pessimistic pronouncements, character assassinations, and nasty case notes. Form your own impressions, and look out for theory countertransference.

4. *Cultivate a "beginner's mind."* It is often observed that therapists just starting out in the field enjoy better outcomes than seasoned clinicians. Experience is a two-edged sword. One may gain practice confidence at the expense of enthusiasm, flexibility, and openness. Remember: "In the beginner's mind there are many possibilities; in the expert's mind there are few."—D.T. Suzuki.

5. *Remember that these clients can and do change.* Long-term follow-up of chronic schizophrenics shows that 50–60%

return to normal or are significantly improved as they get older (Harding & Brooks, 1984; Harding, Zubin, & Strauss, 1987).

SPECIFIC PRINCIPLES

1. *Determine the "customer" for therapy.* Know your client. The person sitting across from you may or may not be your "customer." Your customer may actually be a family member, judge, agency, and so on. Finding out what the *customer* wants to be different helps set the compass for your questions and interventions.

2. *Acknowledge your clients' point of view.* A basic need of people, regardless of their mental status, is to be understood. Empathy, appreciation, genuineness, and trustworthiness are powerful allies in your work with a chronic or "disturbed" person. Clients may be hearing voices or believing in outlandish conspiracies, but they still deserve to be respected and to be heard.

Example:

I do not know if the office is bugged. You are welcome to search and then decide if this is an OK place to talk right now.

3. *Ask what the person or the family wants.* Part of acknowledging clients and building a collaborative relationship, even if they are behaving bizarrely, is to ask what they want to be different as a result of visiting with you. Everybody is motivated for something. Find out what the person's goals are for the therapy or consultation. Resist the temptation to know what's best (except in a case of imminent

danger, when you can, for a time, decide what is necessary in order to ensure safety).

Examples:

What brings you here?

How will you know that you've gotten what you came for?

Dr. X asked that you see me, but I'm wondering what you want from our visit together.

You say that the XYZ Agency has really been hassling you. What do you need to do to get them off your back?

4. *Find out the person's strengths, competencies, resources, and interests.* As with any client, learn what the client/family does well. Look for exceptions to their complaints, in the present and past. Discover their vision of a better future for themselves.

Examples:

You said you've always been bothered by the voices. Can you tell me about a time the voices were there but didn't bother you? Or how about a time when, for a little while, you were distracted and didn't really notice the voices?

Tell me about the last time you were tempted to fly off the handle, but kept your cool. How did you do that? What made the difference for you? How did it make the rest of your day go?

Let's pretend that we're watching a videotape of you in the future, at a time when life in your family is going more the way you want it. In as much detail as possible, tell me what I'm seeing, what dialogue I'm picking up.

5. *Think small.* Forget finding The Cure. Holding out for the goal of transforming the client's personality, changing the family's structure, or eliminating the disorder may rob you and the client of real opportunities for small but meaningful change. Start small and collaboratively establish achievable goals that build success. A small change can make a big difference.

6. *Separate the problem from the person.* Sometimes we inadvertently identify the person with his or her disorder or symptoms. We refer to clients as "my borderline" or "the schizophrenic." We and they tend to forget that there is more to them than their problem. One way of reminding ourselves and our clients of their personhood is to externalize and distinguish the problem or symptom from the person in the interview.

Examples:

Schizophrenia really had you and your family on the run for a while there. When did you get wise to the tricks schizophrenia was playing on you?

So hallucinations tried to convince you to quit your job, but this time you stood up to the hallucinations and didn't let them rob you of the progress you've made.

7. *Do inclusive inner work to calm and value the person.* Usually, people who are disturbed and disturbing are caught in some internal and interpersonal binds. They go into a kind of "symptom trance," in which they forget their resources and tend to regress. Using inclusive logic

(both/and) can be helpful to soothe them and help them resolve binds.

Examples:

It's OK to be as close to me and as far away from me as you need to be. And you can be close and far away at the same time.

You can feel agitated and act in a way that serves you well.

Bill has been using these principles in his career and in caring for his wife, who developed a chronic illness some years ago. He is well aware of the invitations to become discouraged and give up in any chronic situation or when the odds are against one. Tim has been specializing in working with CSMI clients for most of his career. He has found that the course of treatment is varied, but persistence, patience, and flexibility are always required.

Connections to the
Work of Others

Kenneth Stewart, Ph.D.

*P*RESENTED IN THIS EPILOGUE *are the thoughts of Ken Stewart, a longtime mentor and friend of Tim. Ken was trained in traditional clinical psychology in the 1950s and 1960s. He has worked as a clinician in psychiatric and educational settings, and has taught and trained mental health professionals for 35 years. In recent years, we have shared thoughts on therapy and theory (usually while translating each other's technical language). Gradually, we learned that our basic attitudes about our work and clients were very similar. Further, in our views of the nature of effective therapies, we discovered more historical connections than we had realized existed. Most importantly, we have come to appreciate, to a greater degree, several valuable elements in some older theoretical perspectives while also identifying ways in which our current views can extend clinicians' helping strategies in their work with tough clients.*

In this epilogue, Ken relates our vision of effective therapy to key elements of earlier traditional and nontraditional theories. Beyond the direct relationships to the works of Erickson (Haley, 1973) and Haley (1963, 1973, 1980) and others embedded in the preceding chapters, Ken views our work as also mirroring concepts contained in several earlier humanistic theories that focus on the self.

ATTITUDINAL ELEMENTS AND PSYCHOSOCIAL PERSPECTIVES

Behind the clinical applications described in Tim and Bill's work are attitudes and psychosocial views similar to those expressed in the early writings of such legendary clinicians as Adler and Rogers. Like Adler, they view humans as purposeful and yet acknowledge that an individual's capacity to overcome basic problems is powerfully affected by social context, the building/rebuilding of social interest, and the learning/relearning of more effective social interactions. Their work echoes Rogers's deep respect for the fundamental worth of each person and his view that all individuals, even "damaged" individuals, have the capacity to change in those ways that will create a healthier and more congruent life.

As therapists, we emit a constant flow of nonverbal messages that usually are outside our awareness. These messages may or may not be congruent with our verbal messages. In fact, the selection of one specific verbal message to the exclusion of an infinite number of other possible messages can carry with it powerful nonverbal meanings that have far more impact than what we say. These implicit communications often express our deepest attitudes about the people we help, their capacities to change, and our own capacity to help them change.

Tim and Bill, session by session, help clients rebuild and redefine self and relationships in the context of a persistently hopeful therapeutic alliance. In effect, they help their clients create and encode new experiences under distinctive (accepted, safe, hopeful) relationship conditions. Their clients then learn to recreate and generalize these states (new, more effective experiences) to other interpersonal transactions.

Tim and Bill's current work builds on such idealized attitudes as Carl Rogers's "unconditional positive regard" for the person, and complete acceptance of clients' experiencing of their world. Further, Rogers's view that every human being has a core of positive potential (he called it the "actualizing tendency") is a perspective that helps therapists and clients persist in their work together, in the face of extreme and difficult-to-change problems.

Alfred Adler's view of therapy as a partnership, when congruently acted on, also communicates an attitude of acceptance and respect for the person that is an essential element in sustaining hope and in developing self-respect. Tim and Bill's work speaks to the reality that successful helping requires the development of an authentic therapist–client partnership. Believing in the potential strengths and assets of the client, and knowing that the client's potentials are at least as important as the skills and strengths of the therapist, allows the therapist to send congruent nonverbal messages and to select verbal messages that facilitate, rather than hinder, positive change and client growth.

Among existential-humanistic theorists, perhaps James Bugental's (Bugental, 1978) views best express these basic attitudinal elements. His image of therapy as a journey in which the clients are travelers (perhaps seeking new paths for their lives) and the therapist is a guide (and fellow human being) is most consonant with the fundamental attitudes Tim and Bill believe to be crucial.

Taken together, unconditional positive regard, congruent messages, "partnering," and "guiding" attitudes and views carry to the client powerful messages at the conscious and unconscious levels—messages that impact the client's capacity to persist in the face of extremely difficult life problems. Tim and Bill's clinical casework relies heavily on such attitudinal messages.

Maladaptive behavior is neither caused nor eliminated solely by immediate external or social-interpersonal factors. There are individual differences in genetically determined characteristics, neurohormonal and neurophysiological functioning, the individual's unique developmental history and emotional learning, and the self-defining, self-determining channeling of behavior. Discovering the extent to which internal responses, historically learned patterns, and self-definitions can be modified by persistent and clearly targeted problem-centered strategies that focus on current changes in actions and thoughts is the task Tim and Bill set for all therapists working with tough clients.

DISTURBING THE STATUS QUO

There are similarities and connections between Tim and Bill's work and the works of Thomas Szasz (1972). Szasz went beyond the diagnosis of the individual (as "psychotic," and so on) and pointed to the role and functions of institutional psychiatry in the larger social system. Careful reading of his ideas leads one to step outside the role of psychiatrist, psychologist, or social worker in ways that support seeing clients as persons embedded in social systems rather than focusing on their symptoms or diagnostic labels.

His work also supplied us with a hypothesis about our tendency to think in dichotomies (sane/insane; healthy/sick) when faced with a person whose behavior is inconsistent with our perception of the norm. For example, he suggested that we are reassured about our own sanity when we can categorize those who are different from us as "insane." The major problem with dichotomous judgments is that they obscure the potential assets and strengths that exist, especially in severely troubled persons. Such attributions undermine both the persistence of professional helpers and the morale of so-labeled people.

Traditional psychiatric views of the problems of human beings tend to focus on the problematic characteristics of the individual. Psychiatric language, along with the act of psychiatric diagnosis, reinforces and emphasizes the unchanging and fixed qualities of persons. Efforts on behalf of new social and interpersonal learning tend to be neglected in circumstances where the psychiatric/medical view of the person's problems focuses on physiological causes and/or gives no credence to treatments other than drugs. Further, the more difficult the "case," the more attractive are neurophysiological or other physical dysfunctions as explanations—and as reasons not to persist in one's efforts to help.

Such thinking must not be allowed to diminish social/interpersonal intervention efforts. Even if a client suffers physiologically based dysfunctions or limitations, it is essential that therapists persist in their attempts to intervene through the establishment of new perceptions, new behavior, and new social–interpersonal environments in order to discover the client's actual capacity for new adaptations (Parsons & Stewart, 1966). Further, the extent to which such new learning/adaptation may lead to beneficial physiological changes should not be discounted (McClelland, 1989). For Tim and Bill, the "status quo" that needs to be challenged consists of those judgments about chronic or severely disturbed clients that undercut clients' hope and discourage persistent and creative social systems or social-interpersonal interventions by therapists.

LEARNING UNDER EXTREME STRESS

Although strong emotional states have the potential to set the stage for new learning, severe stress frequently results in a person's becoming either disorganized or immobilized. Under conditions of disequilibrium or extreme stress, people often restrict their actions to the most automatic, most overlearned, and least effortful responses.

Effective therapists usually respond in these situations in ways that bring the client "down" emotionally. By reducing disorganization and subsequently using a variety of intervention strategies that focus the client's attention on the most relevant and essential information (often self-meaning-related), they allow the encoding of new, more effective learning and support more effective and adaptive action. However, therapists need to have the flexibility both to lower arousal and, at times, to access and utilize highly aroused states, and, within that intense context, introduce the elements of change. Further, there are occasions when clients should not be brought "down" too quickly because doing so may prevent access to the very information that is needed to help understand and resolve the problem.

A segment of one session within a long-term case will illustrate several aspects of therapeutic work within a "high-arousal," severe disturbance context. At the time, the therapist was relatively inexperienced, having had only about three years as a full-time clinical psychologist in a medical school teaching hospital.

"YOU MEAN I'M NOTHING BUT . . ."

Joan was a highly intelligent, college-age woman who had been hospitalized after various self-damaging actions, including a serious suicide attempt. She was being released from her inpatient status, and a psychiatrist colleague asked me to take over the case for outpatient treatment. The client's self-damaging pattern and personal identity issues were the central problems of focus early in the therapy.

Six sessions into the relationship, I stumbled into a highly intense client reaction precipitated by my confronting the client with the possible meaning of some of her ultimately self-damaging behavior. I had stated, "It appears to me that you act that way to be the opposite of your mother. You're not really being yourself when you just choose to be the opposite of your mother."

In a matter of a few seconds, Joan reflected on the meaning of this statement and then, painfully and increasingly slowly, said, "You . . . mean . . . I'm . . . nothing . . . but . . . a . . . reaction . . . to . . . my . . . mother." She crumbled into a racking, sobbing, shaking, self-absorbed state in which she appeared oblivious to the outside world (a therapist-induced, albeit inadvertent, internal fixation of attention).

As this state continued for several minutes, she became unresponsive to her name and all other efforts to establish contact. In brief, she appeared to be experiencing what I conceptualized then as a dissociative episode. Her level of emotional distress was the most intense I had ever observed. No training had prepared me to deal therapeutically in any specific way with this client's rapid and intense mental and emotional disorganization, nor with her mute and immobilized condition.

Since my confrontational interpretation had resulted in the client's "losing her identity," I intuitively moved to a combination of calm, slow, verbal statements and repeated touch (gently squeezing her arm) in an effort to help. I gently grasped her left wrist and said, "Joan, when I speak to you, you're the one who hears, and when I squeeze your arm, you're the one who feels it. You're the person who is experiencing this. You are more than your reactions to your mother or anyone else." As she made focused eye contact, I said, "You're the one who sees, the person who hears, the person who feels. You're going to be your own person and not just react."

She became increasingly more calm (slower breathing) and less tearful over the next few minutes. When asked if she wanted to continue to work, she answered genuinely, "I don't know what happened and I'm totally exhausted," I responded, "OK, we won't work any more today. We'll just sit here and relax a while until you feel you're ready to go. We can talk about today anytime you like, in our future sessions."

In subsequent weeks, Joan occasionally stated, "I don't really know what happened in that session, but I know something really important took place." I did not analyze, choosing to respond instead with such statements as, "I think the most important thing that happened was that you began to work on becoming your own person." Over the course of the remaining months of our work together, Joan did begin to establish her own personhood and there was only one further self-damaging incident (under the influence of alcohol during a "celebration/party" that coincided with the loss of a significant relationship).

LOOKING BACK WITH A NEW PERSPECTIVE

At the time of the above case, the therapist did not have available to him the types of concepts Tim and Bill write about and certainly was not thinking of purposefully accessing and utilizing intense emotional states. Nonetheless, looking back, that is what he did, and those actions were the most significant interventions that occurred during therapy. The basic point is that highly significant learning took place (largely at an unconscious level) while the client was intensely emotional and highly disorganized. Had the interventions focused solely on "bringing the client down" or, alternatively, rehospitalizing her because she was so severely disorganized, the therapeutic opportunity would have been foreclosed.

Furthermore, the therapist has shifted his attitude concerning this young woman's extreme self-damaging actions. The referring psychiatrist and the therapist, at the time, tended to label this client's actions with such terms as "acting out" and "impulsively suicidal." In contrast, now, her self-damaging and extreme behaviors are viewed as ways for her to have a more autonomous sense of self and some degree of control and power over her life. As also would be the case now for Tim and Bill, the search for healthier self-enhancing alternatives in the face of her severe distress and disorganization was the most central therapeutic challenge.

DISSOCIATION, ANXIETY, AND THE SELF

The idea that strong internal stimuli (altered psychophysiological states often defined as emotions) create a distinctive condition that results in "state-dependent" learning can also be explored in relation to other distinctive "state" stimuli. Self-states appear to be particularly apt vehicles for distinctive and influential associations.

Strong conditions of psychobiological arousal or emotions that arise in circumstances signaling implications for the sense of self frequently prove to be a most important context for effective approaches to treatment. A long line of influential therapists—for example, modern analytic (Kohut), neo-analytic (Horney), interpersonal (Sullivan), humanistic (Rogers), and social learning (Bandura)—have included self-meanings as factors that are critical to the therapeutic process. The term self-states refers to experiences in which self-defining or self-valuing meanings and feelings are prominent elements.

Close reading of Tim and Bill's casework demonstrates their near-constant attention to self-attributions.

Anxiety, defined by Sullivan as the most central and problematic neurophysiological arousal state, is embedded in and results from social meanings experienced in relation to the self. Extreme anxiety-producing experiences that are accompanied by lack of satisfaction of basic needs are often dissociated (Fisher, 1971). In effect, some experiences are not integrated into the self and become dissociated as "not me." Less severe social-rejection/anxiety-laden experiences are typically not dissociated and become integrated into that component of the self that Sullivan labeled the "bad me."

Nonanxious, satisfying experiences make up Sullivan's "good me." Most importantly, for Sullivan, all anxiety experiences, from mild to severe, are tied directly to evaluative, negative self-meanings. Further, these negative self-meanings fall along a continuum in terms of accessibility to one's awareness; those associated with lesser anxiety are more easily accessed than those embedded in more extreme anxiety experiences.

Angyal (1961), in contrast, treated the self as made up of hierarchical organizations that channel subordinate experiences, emotions, and actions. In all persons, two basic self-organizations are developed: a healthy self and an unhealthy ("sick") self. In troubled ("neurotic") persons, the unhealthy self predominates, and the healthy self is underdeveloped and rarely guides the person's experiences and behavior. Angyal's image of personality organization suggests that when one self is being experienced, the other self is, in a sense, dissociated and not experienced.

In the same way that we apply dichotomous thinking to our images of others, Angyal sees us as organizing our experiences and our sense of self in an either–or manner. Further, the development and strengthening of a healthy self-organization is the key to healthy, adaptive lives. Angyal described important treatment concepts in relation to the intrapersonal self-structures of "neurotic" persons. Tim and Bill pay substantial attention to the self-definitions of their chronic and severe tough clients.

Rogers (in Koch, 1961) presented a model of the self-concept that describes states of extreme incongruity between experience and the self-view; in circumstances involving severe anxiety, these states result in dissociated experiences and actions. Extreme instances of sudden, threatening exposure to experiences that contradict the conscious self-concept are described as leading to disorganized behavior that, to the observer, appears removed from the reality of the person's actual "self."

In Tim and Bill's work, such moments are opportunities for important new learning. For the new learning to be positive and beneficial, they attempt to develop and use the supportive security and power of therapeutic social-interpersonal relationships. In much of this work, the unconditional acceptance of the whole person, including the client's previously rejected experiences, becomes a critical element.

The common thread in the works described above is the combination of self-structure concepts and the strong anxiety/emotion episodes that are used to describe or explain the development of dissociated states and other "maladaptive" behavior. Relationships between and among problem-focused therapy, self-states, and anxiety/physiological arousal states clearly need further study and specification.

The perspective underlying the therapeutic interventions described in this book can serve as a vehicle for the suggested further study. As problem-focused concepts are penetrated by self-structure and self-state concepts in future work, an even larger context for the development of integrative treatment strategies will be created.

COMPARISONS TO MORE RECENT PERSPECTIVES

Greenberg and Saffran (1989) present a viewpoint in which emotions are the central focus in psychotherapy. They include the accessing of state-dependent core beliefs as one of five basic change process elements that cut across a variety of theoretical perspectives. As with Rossi's state-dependent views, Greenberg and Saffran's concepts offer a solid base for extending and relating physical-emotional levels to self-meaning levels of helping. Tim and Bill's cases consistently present an image of therapists who create relationships in which clients feel allied, accepted, safe, and supported, a condition that is critical to success, according to Greenberg and Saffran.

Much of the important emotional learning that takes place is a direct result of the meanings about life, self, and others, which are being communicated through our relationship contexts, especially via our "significant other's" indirect communication of attitudes, expectations, and beliefs. Tim and Bill present this indirect, contextual, relationship learning as a coequal partner with their more direct restructuring or reframing of action tendencies and cognitions.

Why is it that so many capable clinicians and influential theorists have developed such vastly different views of human nature, healing, and psychotherapy, all of which make sense of their followers and advocates? And why is it that, for most of these approaches, there is clinical research evidence that shows important and helpful outcomes? Why do most psychologists in the United States currently categorize themselves as eclectic in their work?

Perhaps the fundamental answer to all of these questions is found in the complexity of the human organism and the bidirectional and circular nature of causality and healing in human behavior, especially in social-interpersonal contexts.

In simplest terms, there is so much going on within and between people, even in very brief moments of time, that the observer/clinician/theorist/explainer cannot capture and understand all of the important dimensions or events. Even so, changes along any dimension tend to impact the other dimensions of thought, feeling, and action.

Clinicians select some events and sequences, interpret those within their existing cognitive structures, and, over time, create new theories or explanations. Observations and explanations are always less than the reality of the person and family, and always different from their reality as they experience it. And yet, therapists' observations and explanations create new realities for the client. We give our view(s) back to them (in one or another way), and this act has the potential to change their experience of themselves to varying degrees. Innumerable, varied explanations, each focusing on different dimensions of living (all incomplete) can have an influential impact on the person or family being helped, especially in a relationship with sufficient trust, credibility, and social influence.

Vastly extending the complexity of the helping relationship is the fact that individuals and families also observe, select, interpret, and explain their own behavior and experience, and their own explanations are always less than the total reality of their lives and experiences. And yet an individual's and family's self-explanations are usually more real to them than the outside observer's "total reality!" Thus, the client's self-explanations, explicit and implicit, always meet face-to-face with the clinician's observations, explanations, and interpretations (again, both explicit and implicit). Negotiating the differences between these two territories of subjective experience is at the very heart of establishing the cooperative alliance needed for effective work. Heinssen et al. (1995) have recently described a four-stage model of therapeutic contracting with seriously mentally ill persons.

In addition, to establish effective working alliances, therapists need to appreciate deeply the significance of the nonverbal communications of clients. The significance of attending to nonverbal communication and of establishing solidly coordinated nonverbal interactions in the relationship-building phases of short- and long-term therapy is now beginning to find a research base in the developmental studies of such writers as Tronick (1989). Ericksonian therapists, of course, will say they have known the importance of coordinated nonverbal interactions for many years! Tim and Bill pay serious attention to this dimension in their therapeutic work.

Like Erickson, Tim and Bill emphasize individual uniqueness and further argue for the greater importance of the uniqueness of the individual, the couple, or the family, in their own social contexts, over theoretical generalizations or labels. Yet, they conceptualize client problems in useful ways that guide treatment while not allowing theory to overshadow their awareness of the uniqueness of their clients. In the earlier chapters of this book, Tim and Bill present balanced ideas that allow room both for useful conceptualization and for the discovery of client uniqueness. This was done through such bidirectional concepts as theory evoking change/change evoking theory and meaning creating behavior/behavior creating meaning. Bandura (1989) uses a similar approach when he invokes the "model of reciprocal causation" in discussing the bidirectional relationship between people and their environment.

Masterpasqua (1989) argued for a "competence" model as an alternative to prevailing mental health models. He suggested that neither the traditional medical model nor the currently popular cognitive-rationalist models offer as sufficient a basis for psychological practice as does a competence model embedded in modern evolutionary theory and current clinical research. At the center of psychological adjustment, in Masterpasqua's view, is a competent self that is perceived by the individual as able to cope with the existing and near-term circumstances of one's life. Masterpasqua's definition of competence integrates many dimensions of human functioning about which Tim and Bill have been writing in this book. He writes:

> On the one hand, the ultimate source of a person's ongoing ability to adjust is the (usually automatic) appraisal that he or she has the requisite abilities to meet environmental demands. On the other hand, those self-perceptions and expectations must be continually fed by a lifelong acquisition of adaptive behaviors, cognitions, and relations. Individuals construct out of their assessments of their abilities a self that they believe to be more or less able to meet the challenges of living. Thus, competence can be defined as adaptive cognitive, emotional, behavioral, and social attributes, complemented by the person's implicit or explicit beliefs and expectations about his or her access to and ability to implement those attributes. (p. 1366)

Bednar, Wells, and Peterson (1989) and Bednar and Peterson (1995) have described in depth a parallel perspective using self-esteem as the central concept around which clinical assessment and therapeutic interventions revolve. In their work, coping responses are viewed as crucial for positive self-evaluations. In contrast, avoidance behavior is seen as regularly and automatically being accompanied by damage to one's self-esteem. Their position is consistent with Masterpasqua's view that establishing a soild felt-sense of personal competence is a critical therapeutic goal. They suggest that accomplishing this goal will be realized through clients' learning to cope and, especially, learning not to avoid either life's problems or the painful self-meanings that accompany one's problematic choices.

For Tim and Bill's clients, repeated contacts and extensive experiencing of the therapist as a consistently accepting person were required for trust to develop. More importantly, many repeated opportunities to establish a different, more positive sense of self as well as a sense of their own capacity to function competently (even in the face of failures and nonsupportive relationships) were offered to these clients to help them create resource states that could be carried with them into their new life experiences.

Much of Tim and Bill's work, in fact, is directed toward the establishment, or reestablishment, of a competent self and a solid felt-sense of personal efficacy. The core attribute to a competent person is a sufficient level of self-esteem and self-appreciation to enable the weathering of failures, frustrations, social-interpersonal rejections, and losses—while maintaining the capacity to continue to meet life as a challenge worth pursuing. Creating social, family, and therapeutic conditions that support and encourage the development of "competent selves" is our most important job as mental health professionals, as parents, as family members, and as friends.

REFERENCES

American Psychiatric Association. (1994). *Diagnostic and statistical manual of mental disorders* (4th ed.). Washington, DC: Author.

Anderson, C. M., Reiss, D., & Hogarty, B. (1986). *Schizophrenia and the family.* New York: Guilford Press.

Andrews, J. (1989, May). Integrating visions of reality: Interpersonal diagnosis and the existential vision. *American Psychologist, 44*(5), 803–817.

Angyal, A. (1965). *Neurosis and treatment: A holistic theory.* New York: Wiley.

Bandura, A. (1989, September). Human agency in social cognitive theory. *American Psychologist, 44*(9), 1175–1184.

Bednar, R., & Peterson, S. R. (1995). *Self-esteem: Paradoxes and innovations in clinical theory and practice.* Washington, DC: American Psychological Association.

Bugental, J. F. T. (1978). *Psychotherapy and processs: The fundamentals of an existential-humanistic approach.* MA: Addison-Wesley.

Fischer, W. F. (1970). *Theories of anxiety.* New York: Harper & Row.

Fish, J. (1974). *Placebo therapy.* San Francisco: Jossey-Bass.

Greenberg, L., & Safran, J. (1989, January). Emotion in psychotherapy. *American Psychologist, 44*(1), 19–29.

Haley, J. (1963). *Strategies of psychotherapy.* New York: Grune and Stratton.

Haley, J. (1973). *Uncommon therapy: The psychiatric techniques of Milton H. Erickson.* New York: Norton.

Haley, J. (1980). *Leaving home.* New York: McGraw-Hill.

Harding, C. M., & Brooks, G. W. (1984). Life assessment of a cohort of chronic schizophrenics discharged twenty years ago. In S. Mednick, M. Harway, & K. Finello (Eds.), *The handbook of longitudinal research* (Vol. 2). New York: Praeger.

Harding, C. M., Zubin, J., & Strauss, J. S. (1987). Chronicity in schizophrenia: Fact, partial fact or artifact. *Hospital and Community Psychiatry, 38*(5), 477–484.

Heinssen, R., Levendusky, P., & Hunter, R. (1995, July). Client as colleague: Therapeutic contracting with the seriously mentally. *American Psychologist, 50*(7), 522–532.

Herman, J. (1992). *Trauma and recovery.* New York: Basic Books.

Hunter, R. (1995, July). Benefits of competency-based treatment programs. *American Psychologist, 50*(7), 509–513.

Kardiner, A., & Spiegel, H. (1947). *War, stress and neurotic illness* (Rev. ed.). New York: Hoeber.

Kreisman, J., & Straus, H. (1991). *I hate you—Don't leave me: Understanding borderline personality.* New York: Avon Books.

Madanes, C. (1981). *Strategic family therapy.* San Francisco: Jossey-Bass.

Masterpasqua, F. (1989, November). A competence paradigm for psychological practice. *American Psychologist, 44*(11), 1366–1371.

McClelland, D. (1989, April). Motivational factors in health and disease. *American Psychologist, 44*(4), 675–683.

McFarlane, W. R. (1991). Family psychoeducational treatment. In A. S. Gurman & D. P. Kniskern (Eds.), *Handbook of family therapy* (Vol. 2). New York: Brunner/Mazel.

O'Hanlon, B. (1994, November/December). The third wave. *Family Therapy Network.*

O'Hanlon, B., & Weiner-Davis, M. (1989). *In search of solutions: A new direction in psychotherapy.* New York: Norton.

O'Hanlon, B., & Wilk, J. (1987). *Shifting contexts: The generation of effective psychotherapy.* New York: Guilford Press.

Parsons, O., & Stewart, K. (1966). Effects of supportive versus disinterested interviews on perceptual-motor performance in brain-damaged and neurotic patients. *Journal of Consulting Psychology, 30*(3), 260–266.

Rogers, C. (1959). A theory of therapy, personality, and interpersonal relationships, as developed in the client-centered framework. In S. Koch (Ed.), *Psychology: A study of a science.* New York: McGraw-Hill.

Szasz, T. (1970). *The manufacture of madness.* New York: Harper & Row.

Tronick, E. (1989, February). Emotions and emotional communication in infants. *American Psychologist, 44*(2), 112–119.

White, M., & Epston, D. (1989/1991). *Narrative means to therapeutic ends.* New York: Norton.

INDEX